S0-ATY-254

# Who Should Read This Book?

We've all heard the scenario: the family on vacation stops at a road-side "dig your own" gem mine. Junior finds a sapphire the size of a peach and ends up on national television telling the world how he will spend his fortune.

*T* This book is for those who have read these stories and want their chance to find their own fortune. It is also a book for those who would enjoy the adventure of finding a few gems, getting them cut or polished, and making their own jewelry. It is a book for those people who want to plan a gem hunting vacation with their family. It is a book for those who study the metaphysical properties of gems and minerals and would like to add to their personal collections.

*T* This book is for those who would like to keep the art of rock-hounding alive and pass it on to their children. It is a book on where to find your own gems and minerals and on how to begin what for many is a lifelong hobby.

*T* This is a book for those who aren't interested in the "hidden treasure map through mosquito-infested no-man's-land" approach to treasure hunting but do want to find gems and minerals. It is for those who want to get out the pick and shovel and get a little dirty. (Although at some mines they bring the buckets of pre-dug dirt to you at an environmentally temperature controlled sluicing area.)

Many an unsuspecting tourist has stopped at a mine to try his or her luck and become a rockhound for life. Watch out! Your collection may end up taking the place of your car in your garage.

Good hunting!

# This volume is one in a four-volume series.

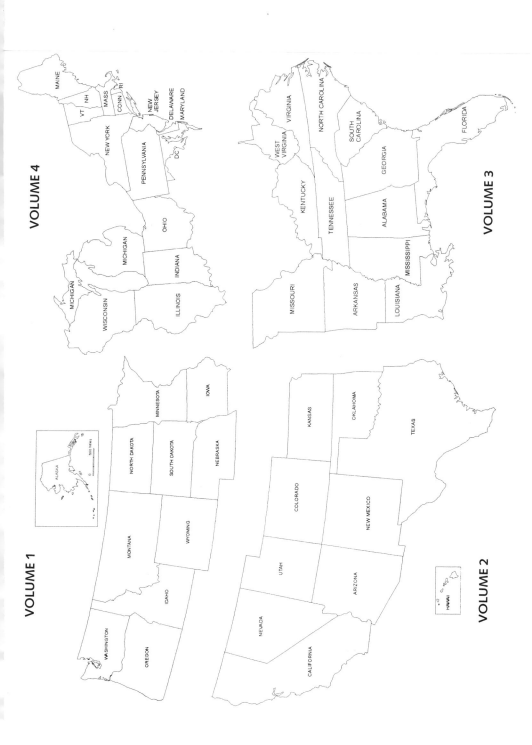

VOLUME 4

VOLUME 3

VOLUME 1

VOLUME 2

*The Treasure Hunter's*

# GEM & MINERAL
# GUIDES TO THE U.S.A.

3RD EDITION

## Where & How to Dig, Pan, and Mine
## Your Own Gems & Minerals

VOLUME 1: NORTHWEST STATES

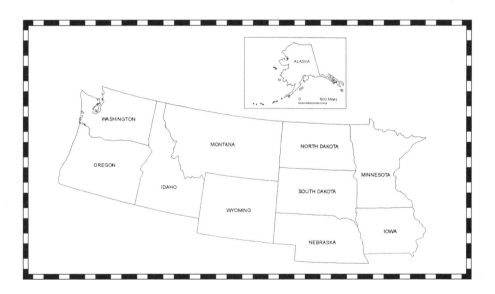

by KATHY J. RYGLE AND STEPHEN F. PEDERSEN
Preface by Antoinette Matlins, P.G.,
author of *Gem Identification Made Easy*

GEMSTONE PRESS
Woodstock, Vermont

*The Treasure Hunter's Gem & Mineral Guides to the U.S.A.:* 3rd Edition
*Where & How to Dig, Pan and Mine Your Own Gems & Minerals*
Volume 1: Northwest States

2006 Third Edition
© 2006 by Kathy J. Rygle and Stephen F. Pedersen
2003 Second Edition
1999 First Edition

Preface © 2006 by Antoinette Matlins

All rights reserved. No part of this book may be reproduced or transmitted in any form or by any means, electronic or mechanical, including photocopying, recording, or by any information storage and retrieval system, without permission in writing from the publisher.

For information regarding permission to reprint material from this book, please mail or fax your request in writing to GemStone Press, Permissions Department, at the address / fax number listed below, or e-mail your request to permissions@gemstonepress.com.

**The Library of Congress has cataloged the second edition as follows:**

Rygle, Kathy J., 1955–
Southwest treasure hunter's gem & mineral guide : where & how to dig, pan, and mine your own gems & minerals / Kathy J. Rygle and Stephen F. Pedersen—2nd ed.
p.     cm.
Rev. ed. of: The treasure hunter's gem & mineral guides to the U.S.A. c1999.
Includes index.
ISBN 0-943763-37-1 (NW)—ISBN 0-943763-40-1 (SE)—
ISBN 0-943763-38-X (SW)—ISBN 0-943763-39-8 (NE)
1.     Minerals—Collection     and     preservation—United     States—Guidebooks.
2.     Precious     stones—Collection     and     preservation—United     States—Guidebooks.
3. United States—Guidebooks. I. Pedersen, Stephen F., 1948– II. Rygle, Kathy J., 1955– Treasure hunter's gem & mineral guides to the U.S.A. III. Title.
QE375.R92 2003
549.973—dc21

2003040801

ISBNs for third edition:
ISBN-13: 978-0-943763-48-4(NW)      ISBN-13: 978-0-943763-50-7(SW)
ISBN-10: 0-943763-48-7(NW)       ISBN-10: 0-943763-50-9(SW)
ISBN-13: 978-0-943763-49-1(NE)      ISBN-13: 978-0-943763-51-4(SE)
ISBN-10: 0-943763-49-5(NE)       ISBN-10: 0-943763-51-7(SE)

Cover design by Bronwen Battaglia
Text design by Chelsea Dippel

10  9  8  7  6  5  4  3  2  1

Manufactured in the United States of America

Published by GemStone Press
A Division of LongHill Partners, Inc.
Sunset Farm Offices, Route 4, P.O. Box 237
Woodstock, VT 05091
Tel: (802) 457-4000      Fax: (802) 457-4004
www.gemstonepress.com

*Dedications, with love, to our parents and children:*

To my parents, Joe and Helen Rygle, who taught me the love of nature; my earliest remembrances of "rockhounding" are hikes with my dad in the fields, forests, and streams near our home. I also remember weekend trips with my mother to a shop that sold specimens of minerals from around the world. To my daughter, Annie Rygle, who shares with me and continues to show me the wonders of nature. Also, thanks to Annie for helping me sort the information for the updates. —K. J. R.

To my parents, Cliff and Leone Pedersen, who taught me to value nature and to not quit. To my daughters Kristi and Debbie, who challenge me to keep growing. —S. F. P.

To our combined families, including Georgia Pedersen, and to family no longer with us.

*With special thanks:*

To all the owners of fee dig mines and guide services, curators and staff of public and private museums, mine owners, and miners. Our thanks to all those individuals both past and present who share the wonders of the earth with us.

To our agent, Barb Doyen, and her childhood rock collection.

To our publisher, Stuart M. Matlins, editor Emily Wichland, and all the staff at GemStone Press for their guidance, assistance, and patience.

To Mrs. Betty Jackson for, in her own way, telling Kathy to write the book.

To God and the wonders He has given us.

And finally, to each other, with love and the perseverance to keep on trying.

# Volume 1—Northwest States

## CONTENTS

# All-American Gems

*by Antoinette Matlins, P.G.*

When Americans think of costly and fabled gems, they associate them with exotic origins—Asia, South Africa or Brazil. They envision violent jungle quests or secret cellars of a sultanate, perhaps scenes from a Jorge Amado novel or from *A Thousand and One Nights*, a voluptuous Indian princess whose sari is adorned with the plentiful rubies and sapphires of her land, or a Chinese emperor sitting atop a throne flanked by dragons carved from exquisitely polished jade.

Asked what gems are mined in the United States, most Americans would probably draw a blank. We know our country is paved with one of the finest highway systems in the world, but we don't know that just below the surface, and sometimes on top of it, is a glittering pavement of gemstones that would color Old Glory. The red rubies of North Carolina, the white diamonds of Arkansas, the blue sapphires of Montana—America teems with treasures that its citizens imagine come from foreign lands. These include turquoise, tourmaline, amethyst, pearls, opals, jade, sapphires, emeralds, rubies, and even gem-quality diamonds.

Not only does America have quantity, it has quality. American gems compare very favorably with gems from other countries. In fact, fine gemstones found in the U.S. can rival specimens from anywhere else in the world. Some gems, like the luxurious emerald-green hiddenite and steely blue benitoite, are found only in America. Others, like the tourmalines of Maine and California, rival specimens found in better-known locations such as Brazil and Zambia.

The discovery of gemstones in U.S. terrain has been called a lost chapter in American history. It continues to be a saga of fashion and fable that, like the stones themselves, are a deep part of our national heritage. Appreciation of our land's generous yield of sparkling colored stones reached a zenith at the end of the nineteenth century with the art nouveau movement and its utilization of them. When the Boer Wars ended, South Africa's diamonds and platinum eclipsed many of our own then so-called semiprecious stones. Not until the 1930s, and again starting with the 1960s, did economics and the yen for color make gems more desirable again.

In the late 1800s, the nation sought out and cherished anything that was unique to the land. The search for gemstones in America coincided with the exploration of the West, and nineteenth-century mineralogists, some bonafide and others self-proclaimed, fulfilled that first call for "Made in America." Their discoveries created sensations not only throughout America but in the capitals of Europe and as far away as China. The Europeans, in fact, caught on before the Americans, exhibiting some of America's finest specimens in many of Europe's great halls.

But the search for gemstones in this country goes back even further than the nineteenth century. In 1541, the Spanish explorer Francisco Coronado trekked north from Mexico in the footsteps of Cortés and Pizarro, searching not only for gold but also for turquoise, amethyst and emeralds. In the early 1600s, when English settlers reached Virginia, they had been instructed "to searche for gold and such jeweles as ye may find."

But what eluded the Spanish explorers and early settlers was unearthed by their descendants. Benitoite, which may be our nation's most uniquely attractive gem, was discovered in 1907 in California's San Benito River headwaters. A beautiful, rare gem with the color of fine sapphire and the fire of a diamond, benitoite is currently found in gem quality only in San Benito, California.

Like many of America's finest stones discovered during the "Gem Rush" of the nineteenth century, benitoite was held in higher regard throughout the rest of the world than it was on its native U.S. soil.

The gem occurs most commonly in various shades of blue. A fine-quality blue benitoite can resemble fine blue sapphire, but it is even more brilliant. It has one weakness, however: in comparison to sapphire, it is relatively soft. It is therefore best used in pendants, brooches and earrings, or in rings with a protective setting.

While benitoite is among the rarest of our gems, our riches hardly stop there. America is the source of other unusual gems, including three even more uniquely American stones, each named after an American: kunzite, hiddenite and morganite.

The story of all-American kunzite is inseparable from the achievements of two men: Charles Lewis Tiffany, founder of Tiffany & Co., and Dr. George Frederick Kunz, world-renowned gemologist. By seeking, collecting and promoting gems found in America, these two did more for the development of native stones than anyone else during, or since, their time.

While working for Tiffany in the late 1800s, Dr. Kunz received a package in the mail containing a stone that the sender believed to be an unusual tourmaline. The stone came from an abandoned mine at Pala Mountain, California, where collectors had found traces of spodumene—a gemstone prized by the ancients but which no one had been able to find for many years. Dr. Kunz was ecstatic to find before him a specimen of "extinct spodumene of a gloriously lilac color." A fellow gemologist, Dr. Charles Baskerville, named the find "kunzite" in his honor.

Kunzite has become a favorite of such designers as Paloma Picasso, not only because of its distinctive shades—lilac, pink, and yellow-green orchid—but because it is one of a diminishing number of gems available in very large sizes at affordable prices. It is a perfect choice for the centerpiece around which to create a very bold, dramatic piece of jewelry. Designer Picasso's creations include a magnificent necklace using a 400-carat kunzite. Although it is a moderately hard stone, kunzite is easily fractured, and care must be taken to avoid any sharp blows.

Kunzite's sister gem, hiddenite, is also a truly "all-American" stone. In 1879, William Earl Hidden, an engraver and mineralogist, was sent to North Carolina on behalf of the great American inventor and prospector Thomas Alva Edison to search for platinum. Hidden found none of the precious white metal but in his pursuit unearthed a new green gemstone, which was named "hiddenite" in his honor.

Less well known than kunzite, hiddenite is an exquisite, brilliant emerald-green variety of spodumene not found anyplace else in the world. While light green and yellow-green shades have been called hiddenite, the Gemological Institute of America—this country's leading authority on gemstones—considers only the emerald-green shade of spodumene, found exclusively in the Blue Ridge Mountains of Mitchell County, North Carolina, to be true hiddenite.

The foothills of the Blue Ridge Mountains also possess America's most significant emerald deposits. While output is minimal compared to Colombia, Zambia or Pakistan, the Rist Mine in Hiddenite, North Carolina, has produced some very fine emeralds, comparable to Colombian stones. The discovery was first made by a farmer plowing his field who found them lying loose on the soil. The country folk, not knowing what they had come across, called the stones "green bolts."

In August 1970, a 26-year-old "rock hound" named Wayne Anthony found a glowing 59-carat "green bolt" at the Rist Mine only two feet from the surface. It was cut into a 13.14-carat emerald of very fine color. Tiffany & Co. later purchased the stone and called it the Carolina Emerald. "The gem is superb," said Paul E. Desautels, then the curator of mineralogy at the Smithsonian Institution. "It can stand on its own merits as a fine and lovely gem of emerald from anywhere, including Colombia." In 1973, the emerald became the official state stone of North Carolina.

A California prize, the warm peach- or pink-shaded morganite, was named by Dr. Kunz for financier John Pierpont Morgan, who purchased the Bement gem collection for donation to the American Museum of Natural History in New York, where it can be viewed today. Morganite is a member of the beryl family, which gives us aquamarine (the clear blue variety of beryl) and emerald (the deep green variety of beryl). However, morganite is available in much larger sizes than its mineralogical cousins and is much more affordable.

Many consider the core of our national treasure chest to be gems like the tourmalines of Maine and California and the sapphires of Montana, gems that are mined in commercial quantities and have earned worldwide reputations. One day in the fall of 1820, two young boys, Ezekiel Holmes and Elijah Hamlin, were rock hunting on Mount Mica in Oxford County, Maine. On the way home, one of the boys saw a flash of green light coming from underneath an uprooted tree. The find was later identified as tourmaline, and Mount Mica became the site of the first commercial gem mine in the United States. The mine was initially worked by Elijah Hamlin and his brother Hannibal, who later became Abraham Lincoln's vice president.

The colors of the rainbow meld delicately in the tourmalines of Maine, producing some of the finest specimens in the world, rivaling in quality even those from Brazil. A 150-mile strip in central Maine provides shades of apple green, burgundy red and salmon pink, to mention just a few. Some stones are bi-colored.

Miners are kept busy in the Pala district of San Diego County, California, as well. California, in fact, is North America's largest producer of gem-quality tourmaline.

The hot-pink tourmalines, for which California is famous, began to come into greater demand in 1985, as pastel-colored stones became more and more coveted by chic women around the globe. Curiously enough, over one hundred years ago the Chinese rejoiced in the fabulous colors of this fashionable stone. The Empress Dowager of the Last Chinese Imperial Dynasty sent emissaries to California in search of pink tourmalines. She garnished her robes with carved tourmaline buttons and toggles, and started a fad which overtook China. Much of the empress's collection of fine carvings was lost or stolen when the dynasty fell around 1912, but artifacts made from California's pink tourmaline can be seen today in a Beijing museum. China's fascination with pink tourmalines lasted long after the empress. In 1985, a contingent of the Chinese Geological Survey came to California with two requests: to see Disneyland and the Himalaya Mine, original site of California pink tourmaline.

While the Chinese are mesmerized by our tourmalines, Americans have always been attracted to China's jade. But perhaps we ought to take stock of our own. Wyoming, in fact, is the most important producer of the stone in the Western Hemisphere. The state produces large quantities of good-quality green nephrite jade—the type most commonly used in jewelry and carvings. California also boasts some jade, as does Alaska. Chinese immigrants panning for gold in California in the late 1800s found large boulders of nephrite and sent them back to China, where the jade was carved and sold within China and around the world.

The U.S. is also one of the largest producers of turquoise. Americans mostly associate this stone with American Indian jewelry, but its use by mainstream designers has regularly come in and out of fashion.

Some of the most prized gems of America are the stunning sapphires from Yogo Gulch, Montana. These sapphires emit a particularly pleasing shade of pale blue, and are known for their clarity and brilliance.

The Montana mine was originally owned by a gold-mining partnership. In 1895, an entire summer's work netted a total of only $700 in gold plus a cigar box full of heavy blue stones. The stones were sent to Tiffany & Co. to be identified. Tiffany then sent back a check for $3,750 for the entire box of obviously valuable stones.

Once one can conceive of gem-quality sapphires in America, it takes only a small stretch of the mind to picture the wonderful diamonds found here. A 40.23-carat white gem found in Murfreesboro, Arkansas, was cut into a 14.42-carat emerald-cut diamond named Uncle Sam. Other large diamonds include a 23.75-carat diamond found in the mid-nineteenth century in Manchester, Virginia, and a greenish 34.46-carat diamond named the Punch Jones, which was claimed to have been found in Peterstown, West Virginia.

Each year, thousands of people visit Crater of Diamonds State Park in Arkansas, where, for a fee, they can mine America's only proven location of gem-quality diamonds. Among them is a group known as "regulars" who visit the park looking for their "retirement stone."

In 1983, one of the regulars, 82-year-old Raymond Shaw, came across a 6.7-carat rough diamond. He sold it for $15,000 uncut. According to Mark Myers, assistant superintendent of the state park, the stone was cut into an exceptionally fine, 2.88-carat gem (graded E/Flawless by the Gemological Institute of America). Myers says the cut stone, later called the Shaw Diamond, was offered for sale for $58,000.

Diamonds have also been found along the shores of the Great Lakes, in many localities in California, in the Appalachian Mountains, in Illinois, Indiana, Ohio, Kentucky, New York, Idaho and Texas. Exploration for diamonds continues in Michigan, Wisconsin, Colorado and Wyoming, according to the U.S. Bureau of Mines. The discovery of gem-quality diamonds in Alaska in 1986 initiated a comprehensive search there for man's most valued gem.

Many questions concerning this country's store of gems remain unanswered. "Numerous domestic deposits of semiprecious gem stones are known and have been mined for many years," wrote the Bureau of Mines in a 1985 report. "However, no systematic evaluations of the magnitude of these deposits have been made and no positive statements can be made about them." Even as the United States continues to offer up its kaleidoscopic range of gems, our American soil may hold a still greater variety and quantity of gems yet to be unearthed.

And here, with the help of these down-to-earth (in the best possible way!)

guides, you can experience America's gem and mineral riches for yourself. In these pages rockhounds, gemologists, vacationers, and families alike will find a hands-on introduction to the fascinating world of gems and minerals . . . and a treasure map to a sparkling side of America. Happy digging!

*T*

**Antoinette Matlins, P.G.** is the most widely read author in the world on the subject of jewelry and gems (*Jewelry & Gems: The Buying Guide* alone has almost 400,000 copies in print). Her books are published in six languages and are widely used throughout the world by consumers and professionals in the gem and jewelry fields. An internationally respected gem and jewelry expert and a popular media guest, she is frequently quoted as an expert source in print media and is seen on ABC, CBS, NBC and CNN, educating the public about gems and jewelry and exposing fraud. In addition, Matlins is active in the gem trade. Her books include *Jewelry & Gems: The Buying Guide; Jewelry & Gems at Auction: The Definitive Guide to Buying & Selling at the Auction House & on Internet Auction Sites; Colored Gemstones: The Antoinette Matlins Buying Guide—How to Select, Buy, Care for & Enjoy Sapphires, Emeralds, Rubies and Other Colored Gems with Confidence and Knowledge; Diamonds: The Antoinette Matlins Buying Guide—How to Select, Buy, Care for & Enjoy Diamonds with Confidence and Knowledge; Engagement & Wedding Rings: The Definitive Buying Guide for People in Love; The Pearl Book: The Definitive Buying Guide;* and *Gem Identification Made Easy: A Hands-On Guide to More Confident Buying & Selling* (all GemStone Press).

# Introduction

This is a guide to commercially operated gem and mineral mines (fee dig mines) within the United States that offer would-be treasure hunters the chance to "dig their own," from diamonds to thundereggs.

For simplicity, the term *fee dig site* is used to represent all types of fee-based mines or collection sites. However, for liability reasons, many mines no longer let collectors dig their own dirt, but rather dig it for them and provide it in buckets or bags. Some fee-based sites involve surface collection.

This book got its start when the authors, both environmental scientists, decided to make their own wedding rings. Having heard stories about digging your own gems, they decided to dig their own stones for their rings. So off to Idaho and Montana they went, taking their three children, ages 8, 13, and 15 at the time, in search of opals and garnets, their birthstones. They got a little vague information before and during the trip on where to find gem mines and in the process got lost in some of those "mosquito-infested lands." But when they did find actual "dig your own" mines (the kind outlined in this book), they found opals, garnets, and even sapphires. They have since made other trips to fee dig mines and each time have come home with treasures and some incredible memories.

The authors are also now the proud owners of a set of lapidary equipment, i.e., rock saw and rock polisher. They first used them to cut thundereggs collected from a mine in Oregon. The next project was to trim the many pounds of fossil fish rocks they acquired at a fee dig fossil site. The sequel to this guide series will cover authorized fossil collecting sites as well as museums on fossils and dinosaurs. It will include such topics as where to view and even make plaster casts of actual dinosaur tracks. There are even museums where kids of all ages can dig up a full-sized model of a dinosaur!

## Types of Sites

The purpose of this book is principally to guide the reader to fee dig mine sites. These are gem or mineral mines where you hunt for the gem or mineral in ore at or from the mine. At fee dig sites where you are actually permitted to go into the field and dig for yourself, you will normally be shown what the gem or mineral you are seeking looks like in its natural state (much different from the polished or cut stone). Often someone is available to go out in the field with you and show you where to dig. At sites where you purchase gem- or mineral-bearing ore (either native or enriched) for washing in a flume, the process is the same: there will usually be examples of rough stones for comparison, and help in identifying your finds.

Also included are a few areas that are not fee dig sites but that are well-defined collecting sites, usually parks or beaches.

Guided field trips are a little different. Here the guide may or may not have examples of what you are looking for, but he or she will be with you in the field to help in identifying finds.

For the more experienced collector, there are field collecting areas where you are on your own in identifying what you have found. Several fee areas and guided field trips appropriate for the experienced collector are available. Check out the listings for Ruggles Mine (Grafton, NH); Harding Mine (Dixon, NM); Poland Mining Camps (Poland, ME); Perhams (West Paris, ME); and Gem Mountain Quarry Trips (Spruce Pine, NC).

## Knowing What You're Looking For

Before you go out into the field, it is a good idea to know what you are looking for. Most of the fee dig mines listed in this guide will show you specimens before you set out to find your own. If you are using a guide service, you have the added bonus of having a knowledgeable person with you while you search to help you find the best place to look and help you identify your finds.

Included here is a listing of museums that contain rock and gem exhibits. A visit to these museums will help prepare you for your search. You may find examples of gems in the rough and examples of mineral specimens similar to the ones you will be looking for. Museums will most likely have displays of gems or minerals native to the local area. Some of the gems and minerals listed in this guide are of significant interest, and specimens of them can be found in museums around the country. Displays accompanying the exhibits might tell you how the gems and minerals were found, and their place in our nation's history. Many museums also hold collecting field trips or geology programs, or may be able to put you in touch with local rock and lapidary clubs.

For more information on learning how to identify your finds yourself—and even how to put together a basic portable "lab" to use at the sites—the book *Gem Identification Made Easy* by Antoinette Matlins and A. C. Bonanno (GemStone Press) is a good resource.

Rock shops are another excellent place to view gem and mineral specimens before going out to dig your own. A listing of rock shops would be too extensive to include in a book such as this. A good place to get information on rock shops in the area you plan to visit is to contact the chamber of commerce for that area. Rock shops may be able to provide information not only on rockhounding field trips but also on local rock clubs that sponsor trips.

Through mine tours you can see how minerals and gems were and are taken from the earth. On these tours, visitors learn what miners go through to remove the ores from the earth. This will give you a better appreciation for those sparkly gems you see in the showroom windows, and for many of the items we all take for granted in daily use.

You will meet other rockhounds at the mine. Attending one of the yearly events listed in the guide will also give you the chance to meet people who share your interest in gems and minerals and exchange ideas, stories, and knowledge of the hobby.

## How to Use This Guide

To use this book, you can pick a state and determine what mining is available there, or pick a gem or mineral and determine where to go to "mine" it.

In this guide are indexes that will make the guide simple to use. If you are interested in finding a particular gem or mineral, go to the Index by Gem or Mineral in the back of the book. In this index, gems and minerals are listed in alphabetical order with the states and cities where fee dig sites for that gem or mineral may be found.

If you are interested in learning of sites near where you live, or in the area where you are planning a vacation, or if you simply want to know whether there are gems and minerals in a particular location, go to the Index by State, located in the back of the guide. The state index entries are broken down into three categories: Fee Dig Sites/Guide Services, Museums and Mine Tours, and Special Events and Tourist Information.

There are also several special indexes for use in finding your birthstone, anniversary stone, or zodiac stone.

### Site Listings

The first section of each chapter lists fee dig sites and guide services that are available in each state. Included with the location of each site is a description of the site, directions to find it, what equipment is provided, and what you must supply. Costs are listed, along with specific policies of the site. Also included are other services available at the site and information on camping, lodging, etc. in the area of the site. Included in the section with fee dig sites are guide services for collecting gems and minerals.

In the second section of each chapter, museums of special interest to the gem/mineral collector and mine tours available to the public are listed. Besides being wonderful ways to learn about earth science, geology, and mining history (many museums and tours also offer child-friendly exhibits), museums are particularly useful for viewing gems and minerals in their rough or natural state before going out in the field to search for them.

The third section of each chapter lists special events involving gems and minerals, and resources for general tourist information.

A sample of the listings for fee dig mines and guide services (Section 1 in the guides) is on the next page.

## Tips for mining:

1. Learn what gems or minerals can be found at the mine you are going to visit.
2. Know what the gem or mineral that you're hunting looks like in the rough before you begin mining.

Visiting local rock shops and museums will help in this effort.

3. When in doubt, save any stone that you are unsure about. Have an expert at the mine or at a local rock shop help you identify your find.

# Sample Fee Dig Site Listing

**TOWN in which the site is located /** *Native or enriched[1] • Easy, moderate, difficult[2]*

Dig your own *T*

*The following gems may be found:*
- List of gems and minerals found at the mine

Mine name
Owner or contact (where available)
Address
Phone number
Fax
E-mail address
Website address

**Open:** Months, hours, days
**Info:** Descriptive text regarding the site, including whether equipment is provided
**Admission:** Fee to dig; costs for predug dirt
**Other services available**
**Other area attractions** (at times)
**Information on lodging or campground facilities** (where available)
**Directions**

Map (where available)

*Notes:*

1. Native or enriched. *Native* refers to gems or minerals found in the ground at the site, put there by nature. *Enriched* means that gems and minerals from an outside source have been brought in and added to the soil. Enriching is also called "salting"—it is a guaranteed return. Whatever is added in a salted mine is generally the product of some commercial mine elsewhere. Thus, it is an opportunity to "find" gemstones from around the world the easy way, instead of traveling to jungles and climbing mountains in remote areas of the globe. Salted mines are particularly nice for giving children the opportunity to find a wide variety of gems and become involved in gem identification. The authors have tried to indicate if a mine is enriched, but to be sure, ask at the mine beforehand. If the status could not be determined, this designation was left out.

2. Sites are designated as easy, moderate, or difficult. This was done to give you a feel for what a site may be like. You should contact the site and make a determination for yourself if you have any doubts.

*Easy:* This might be a site where the gem hunter simply purchases bags or buckets of predug dirt, washes the ore in a flume or screens the gem-bearing gravel to concentrate the gems, and flips the screen. The gems or minerals are then picked out of the material remaining in the screen. A mine which has set aside a pile of mine material for people to pick through would be another type of site designated as "Easy."

*Moderate:* Mining at a "Moderate" site might mean digging with a shovel, then loading the dirt into buckets, followed by sifting and sluicing. Depending on your knowledge of mineral identification, work at a "Moderate" site might include searching the surface of the ground at an unsupervised area for a gem or mineral you are not familiar with (this could also be considered difficult).

*Difficult:* This might be a site requiring tools such as picks and shovels, or sledgehammers and chisels. The site may be out of the way and/or difficult to get to. Mining might involve heavy digging with the pick and shovel or breaking gems or minerals out of base rock using a sledge or chisel.

---

### Special Note:

Although most museums and many fee dig sites are handicapped accessible, please check with the listing directly.

---

### *Maps*

Maps are included to help you locate the sites in the guide. At the beginning of each state, there is a state map showing the general location of towns where sites are located.

Local maps are included in a listing when the information was available. *These maps are not drawn to scale!* These maps provide information to help you get to the site but are not intended to be a substitute for a road map. Please check directly with the site you are interested in for more detailed directions.

## Fees

Fees listed in these guides were obtained when the book was updated, and may have changed. They are included to give you at least a general idea of the costs you will be dealing with. Please contact the site directly to confirm charges.

Many museums have discounts for members and for groups, as well as special programs for school groups. Please check directly with the institution for information. Many smaller and/or private institutions have no fee, but do appreciate donations to help meet the costs of staying open.

Many sites accept credit cards; some may not. Please check ahead for payment options if this is important.

## Requesting Information by Mail

When requesting information by mail, it is always appreciated if you send a SASE (self-addressed stamped envelope) along with your request. Doing this will often speed up the return of information.

## Equipment and Safety Precautions

### Equipment

The individual sites listed in these guides often provide equipment at the mine. Please note that some fee dig sites place limitations on the equipment you can use at their site. Those limitations will be noted where the information was available. Always abide by the limitations; remember that you are a guest at the site.

On the following pages are figures showing equipment for rockhounding. Figures A and B identify some of the equipment you may be told you need at a site. Figure C shows material needed to collect, package, transport, and record your findings. Figure D illustrates typical safety equipment.

Always use safety glasses with side shields or goggles when you are hammering or chiseling. Chips of rock or metal from your tools can fly off at great speed in any direction when hammering. Use gloves to protect your hands as well.

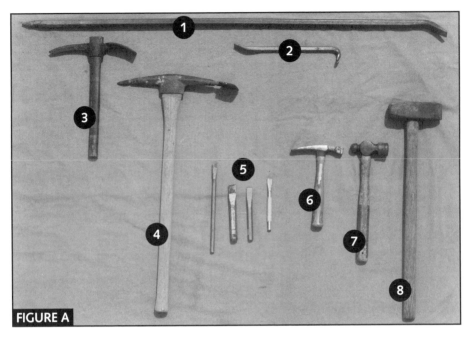

**FIGURE A**

1. Crowbar
2. Pry bar
3. Smaller pick
4. Rock pick
5. Various-sized chisels (*Note:* When working with a hammer and chisel, you may want to use a chisel holder, not shown, for protecting your hand if you miss. Always use eye protection with side shields and gloves!)
6. Rock hammer (*Note:* Always use eye protection.)
7. 3-pound hammer (*Note:* Always use eye protection.)
8. Sledgehammer (*Note:* When working with a sledgehammer, wear hard-toed boots along with eye protection.)

Other useful tools not shown include an ultraviolet hand lamp, and a hand magnifier.

Not pictured, but something you don't want to forget, is your camera and plenty of extra film. You may also want to bring along your video camera to record that "big" find, no matter what it might be.

Not pictured, but to be considered: knee pads and seat cushions.

### Other Safety Precautions

- Never go into the field or on an unsupervised site alone. With protective clothing, reasonable care, proper use of equipment, and common sense,

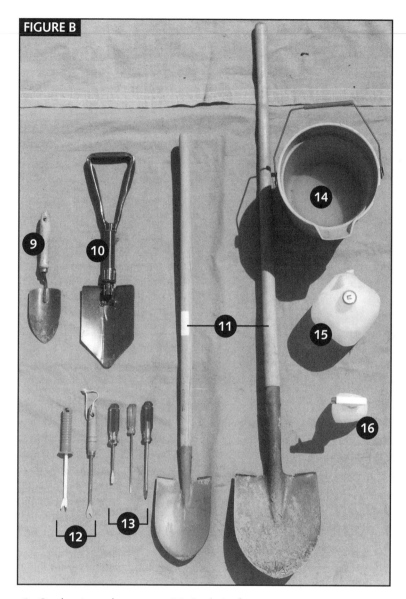

FIGURE B

9. Garden trowel
10. Camp shovel
11. Shovels
12. Garden cultivators
13. Screwdrivers

14. Bucket of water
15. (Plastic) jug of water
16. Squirt bottle of water; comes in handy at many of the mines to wash off rocks so you can see if they are or contain gem material

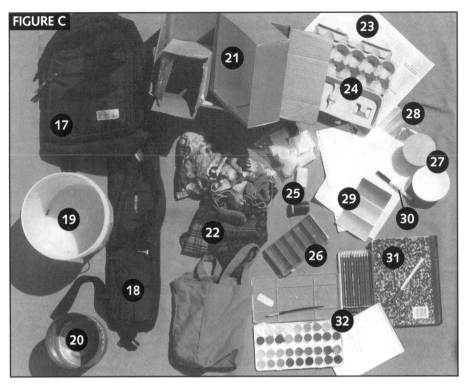

FIGURE C

17. Backpack
18. Waist pack to hold specimens
19. Bucket to hold specimens
20. Coffee can to hold specimens
21. Boxes to pack, transport, and ship specimens
22. Bags—various sized bags to carry collected specimens in the field
23. Newspaper to wrap specimens for transport
24. Egg cartons to transport delicate specimens
25. Empty film canisters to hold small specimens
26. Plastic box with dividers to hold small specimens
27. Margarine containers to hold small specimens
28. Reclosable plastic bags to hold small specimens
29. Gummed labels to label specimens (Whether you are at a fee dig site or with a guide, usually there will be someone to help you identify your find. It is a good idea to label the find when it is identified so that when you reach home, you won't have boxes of unknown rocks.)
30. Waterproof marker for labeling
31. Field log book to make notes on where specimens were found
32. Sketching pencils, sketchbook, paint to record your finds and the surrounding scenery

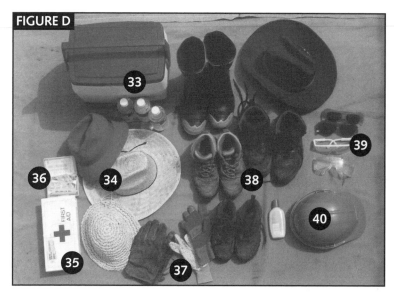

FIGURE D

33. Food and water—always carry plenty of drinking water (*Note:* many sites tell you in advance if they have food and water available or if you should bring some; however, it is always a good idea to bring extra drinking water. Remember—if you bring it in, pack it back out.)

34. Hats. Many of the sites are in the open, and the summer sun can be hot and dangerous to unprotected skin. Check with the site to see if they have any recommendations for protective clothing. Also, don't forget sunscreen.

35. First aid/safety kit

36. Snakebite kit. If the area is known to have snakes, be alert and take appropriate safety measures, such as boots and long pants. (*Note:* while planning our first gem-hunting trip, we read that the first aid kit should contain a snakebite kit. Just like rockhounds, snakes seem to love rocky areas!) In most cases, if you visit sites in the book, you will be either at a

flume provided by the facility, or with an experienced guide. At the first, you will most likely never see a snake; at the second, your guide will fill you in on precautions. For listings where you will be searching on a ranch or state park, ask about special safety concerns such as snakes and insects when you pay your fee. These sites may not be for everyone.

37. Gloves to protect your hands when you are working with sharp rock or using a hammer or chisel

38. Boots—particularly important at sites where you will be doing a lot of walking, or walking on rocks

39. Safety glasses with side shields, or goggles. Particularly important at hard rock sites or any site where you or others may be hitting rocks. Safety glasses are available with tinted lenses for protection from the sun.

40. Hard hats—may be mandatory if you are visiting an active quarry or mine; suggested near cliffs

accidents should be avoided, but in the event of an illness or accident, you always want to have someone with you who can administer first aid and call for or seek help.

- Always keep children under your supervision.
- Never enter old abandoned mines or underground diggings!
- Never break or hammer rocks close to another person!

## Mining Techniques

### How to Sluice for Gems

This is the most common technique used at fee dig mines where you buy a bucket of gem ore (gem dirt) and wash it at a flume.

1. Place a quantity of the gem ore in the screen box, and place the screen box in the water. Use enough gem ore to fill the box about a third.

2. Place the box in the water, and shake it back and forth, raising one side,

Clockwise from top: Gold pan; screen box used for sluicing; screen box used for screening.

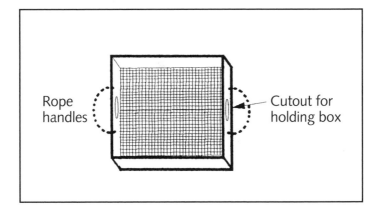

Rope handles

Cutout for holding box

## How to Build a Screen Box

1. A screen box that is easy to handle is generally built from 1" x 4" lumber and window screening.

2. Decide on the dimensions of the screen box you want, and cut the wood accordingly. Dimensions generally run from 12" x 12" up to 18" x 18". Remember that the end pieces will overlap the side pieces, so cut the end pieces 1½" longer.

3. There are two alternative methods of construction. In one, drill pilot holes in the end pieces, and use wood screws to fasten the end pieces to the side pieces. In the other, use angle irons and screws to attach the ends and sides.

4. Cut the screening to be ¼" smaller than the outside dimensions of the screen box, and use staples to attach the screen to the bottom of the box. Use metal screening rather than plastic if possible. For a stronger box, cut ¼" or ⅜" hardware cloth to the same dimensions as the screening, and staple the hardware cloth over the screening. The hardware cloth will provide support for the screening.

5. Cut ¼" wood trim to fit, and attach it to the bottom of the box to cover the edges of the screening and hardware cloth and staples.

6. If you like, add rope handles or cut handholds in the side pieces for easier handling.

then the other, so that the material in the box moves back and forth. What you are doing is making the stones move around in the screen box, while washing dirt and sand out of the mixture.

3. After a minute or two of washing, take the screen box out of the flume, and let it drain. Look through the stones remaining in the screen box for your treasure. If you're not sure about something, ask one of the attendants.

4. When you can't finding anything more, put the box back in the flume and wash it some more, then take it out and search again.

5. If possible, move your screen box into bright light while you are searching, since the gems and minerals often show up better in bright light.

### How to Screen for Gems

This is another common technique used at fee dig mines where you buy a bucket of gem ore and screen it for gems. (The authors used this technique for garnets and sapphires in Montana.)

1. Place a quantity of the gem ore in the screen box, and place the screen box in the water. Use enough gem dirt to fill the box about a third.

2. Place the box in the water, and begin tipping it back and forth, raising one side, then the other, so that the material in the box moves back and forth. What you are doing is making the gemstones, which are heavier than the rock and dirt, move into the bottom center of the screen box while at the same time washing dirt and sand out of the mixture.

3. After a minute or two, change the direction of movement to front and back.

4. Repeat these two movements (Steps 2 and 3) three or four times.

5. Take the box out of the water and let it drain, then place a board on top and carefully flip the box over onto the sorting table. It may be helpful to

put a foam pad in the box, then put the board over it. This helps keep the stones in place when you flip the box. If you have done it right, the gemstones will be found in the center of the rocks dumped onto the board. Use tweezers to pick the rough gemstones out of the rocks, and place them in a small container.

## How to Pan for Gold

The technique for panning for gold is based on the fact that gold is much heavier than rock or soil. Gently washing and swirling the gold-bearing soil in a pan causes the gold to settle to the bottom of the pan. A gold pan has a flat bottom and gently slanting sides. Some modern pans also have small ridges or rings around the inside of the pan on these slanting sides. As the soil is washed out of the pan, the gold will slide down the sides, or be caught on the ridges and stay in the pan. Here's how:

1. Begin by filling the pan with ore, about ⅔ to ¾ full.

2. Put your pan in the water, let it gently fill with water, then put the pan under the water surface. Leave the pan in the water, and mix the dirt around in the pan, cleaning and removing any large rocks.

3. Lift the pan out of the water, then gently shake the pan from side to side while swirling it at the same time. Do this for 20–30 seconds to get the gold settled to the bottom of the pan.

4. Still holding the pan out of the water, continue these motions while tilting the pan so that the dirt begins to wash out. Keep the angle of the pan so that the crease (where the bottom and sides meet) is the lowest point.

5. When there is only about a tablespoon of material left in the pan, put about ½ inch of water in the pan, and swirl the water over the remaining material. As the top material is moved off, you should see gold underneath.

6. No luck? Try again at a different spot.

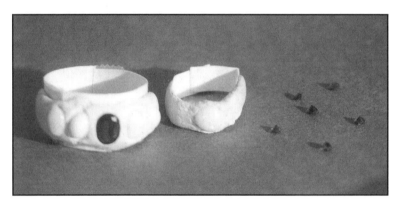

The authors sent their rough gems away for faceting. Using the faceted gems, they made crude mock-ups and sketches of the rings they wanted; then they sent the mock-ups, sketches, and gems to be made into rings.

The finished rings.

## Notes on Gem Faceting, Cabbing, and Mounting Services

Many of the fee dig sites offer services to cut and mount your finds. Quality and costs vary. Trade journals such as *Lapidary Journal* and *Rock & Gem* (available at most large bookstores or by subscription) list suppliers of these services, both in the United States and overseas. Again, quality and cost vary. Local rock and gem shops in your area may offer these services, or it may be possible to work with a local jeweler. Your local rock club may be able to provide these services or make recommendations.

After their first gem-hunting trip, the authors had some of their finds faceted and cabochoned. They then designed rings and had them made using these stones, as shown in the photos on the previous page.

Taking sifted gravel to the jig at a sapphire mine in Montana. Pictured from left to right: Steve, Kathy, Annie Rygle, Debra Pedersen, Kristin Pedersen.

# ALASKA

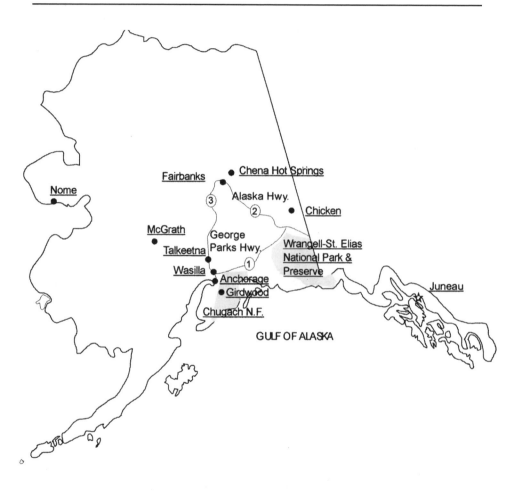

**State Gemstone:** Jade (1968)
**State Mineral:** Gold (1968)

**ANCHORAGE /** *Native • Easy to Moderate*

## Pan, Dig, or Dredge for Gold  *T*

*The following gems or minerals may be found:*

- Gold

State of Alaska
Alaska DNR
Public Information Office
Robert B. Atwood Building
550 W. 7th Avenue, Suite 1260
Anchorage, AK 99501-3557
Phone: (907) 269-8400
Fax: (907) 269-8901
E-mail: pic@dnr.state.ak.us

**Open:** Gold panning areas generally open during daylight hours. DNR office hours are Monday–Friday, 10:00 A.M.–5:00 P.M.

**Info:** The state of Alaska has set aside three areas to provide permanent recreational mining experiences for the general public—these areas are listed below.

**Caribou Creek Recreational Mining Site:** Parking area and trailhead at Mile 104 of the Glenn Highway, just north of Matanuska Glacier. Recreational mining is allowed only within 100 feet of ordinary high water of the creeks. In addition, some areas within this site are under claim, and mining is not allowed in those areas. Allowed mining methods include panning, prospecting, and hand excavating. Suction dredging with a nozzle intake of 6 inches, pumping no more than 30,000 gallons of water per day, is only allowed with a permit from the ADNR. There are no facilities other than an outhouse.

**Hatcher Pass Public Use Area:** Located in the Independence Mine State Historical Park. Take the Glenn Highway, and turn left onto Palmer Fishhook Road approximately two miles north of Palmer. There will be signs for both the park and the public use area. The public use area begins a little before mile 8 on the Palmer Fishhook Road. Some areas within this site are under claim, and mining is not allowed in those areas. Allowed mining methods include panning, prospecting, and hand excavating. Suction dredging with a nozzle intake of 6 inches, pumping no more than 30,000 gallons of water per day, is only allowed with a permit from the ADNR.

**Petersville Recreational Mining Area:** From the Parks Highway, take the Petersville Road at Trapper Creek, (115 miles north of Anchorage). The recreational mining area is about 30 miles from the highway; the last few miles are recommended for four-wheel drive vehicles, ATVs, or similar vehicles, particularly since Peters Creek must be forded in order to reach the recreational mining area. Do not try to ford the creek with a passenger car.

There are no facilities at this area.

**Rates:** No charge for Caribou Creek and Petersville Recreational Mining Areas; there is a $5.00 parking fee for the Independence Mine State Historical Park.

## CHUGACH NATIONAL FOREST /
*Native ▪ Easy to Moderate*

## Pan for Gold  *T*

*The following gems or minerals may be found:*

▪ **Gold**

Chugach National Forest
3301 C Street, Suite 300
Anchorage, AK 99503-3998
Phone: (907) 271-2500
www.akmining.com/mine/chugach.htm

**Open:** Daylight hours for gold panning areas. Call for national forest office hours.
**Info:** Chugach National Forest has 4 designated recreational gold panning areas: Bertha Creek, Crescent Creek, Resurrection Creek, and Sixmile Creek. Their online gold panning brochure has information on specific gold panning areas, as well as guidelines and limitations to be observed. Additional information can be obtained from the national forest office, or from the following:

Minerals Specialist, Seward Ranger District
334 Fourth Avenue
P.O. Box 390
Seward, AK 99664-0390
Phone: (907) 224-3374; or

Minerals Specialist, Glacier Ranger District
Monarch Mine Road
Girdwood, AK 99587
Phone: (907) 783-3242

**Rates:** Free.
**Directions:** Call or check the website for directions.

## COPPER CENTER / *Native ▪ Easy to Moderate*

## Pan for Gold or Hunt for Minerals  *T*

*The following gems or minerals may be found:*

▪ **Gold, any collectible mineral, or rock**

Wrangell-St Elias National Park and Preserve
P.O. Box 439
Copper Center, AK 99573
Phone: (907) 822-5234
E-mail: wrst_interpretation@nps.gov

**Open:** Daylight hours.
**Info:** The national park service allows collection of any rock or mineral except silver, platinum, gemstones, or fossils. Gold panning is allowed, but shovels, sluices, or dredges are not. Metal detectors are illegal in national parks. Also, some areas in the park are under claim, and no mining or collecting is allowed on those claims. Check with the park office for areas under claim.
**Rates:** Free.
**Directions:** Call for directions to park headquarters.

**FAIRBANKS /** *Easy*

## Pan for Gold  *T*

*The following gems or minerals may be found:*

- Gold

El Dorado Gold Mine
1975 Discovery Drive
Fairbanks, AK 99709
Phone: (907) 479-6673; (866) 479-6673
Fax: (907) 479-4613
E-mail: reservations@eldoradogoldmine.com
www.eldoradogoldmine.com

**Open:** Mid-May–mid-September. Tours depart 9:45 A.M. and 3:00 P.M. daily (no morning tours Monday or Saturday).
**Info:** After a short "course" on mining, try your hand at panning for gold. Gold panning is included in the El Dorado Gold Mine tour. See Section 2 for more information on the mine tour.
**Rates:** "Pokes" of pay dirt are provided as part of the tour. See listing under Section 2.
**Other services available:** Ride a narrow-gauge railroad through the past to a working gold mine; walking tour of mining camp; large gold nugget display; airstrip.

**Directions:** Nine miles north of Fairbanks on the Elliott Highway. Located on Highway #2 off Elliott Highway.

**FAIRBANKS /** *Native • Easy to Moderate*

## Pan, Sluice, or Dredge for Gold  *T*

*The following gems or minerals may be found:*

- Gold

Faith Creek Camp
P.O. Box 70929
Fairbanks, AK 99707
Phone: (303) 582-5108 or (907) 347-8373
E-mail: faithcreekcamp@aol.com

**Open:** May 15–September 15.
**Info:** Faith Creek Camp is at the headwaters of the Chatanka River. Pan, sluice, or dredge using your own equipment in one of the richest mining districts in Alaska. You can also rent a dredge, and get training on dredging at the camp.
**Rates:** $40.00/day for any panning, sluicing, or dredging up to a 2-inch dredge. $50.00/day to use a 2½- to 6-inch dredge. $100.00/day to use Faith Creek Camp's dredge, plus dredge set-up fee of $50.00, and $100.00 for a one-hour training.
**Other services available:** Cabins are available for rent, or you can bring your own camper or tent.

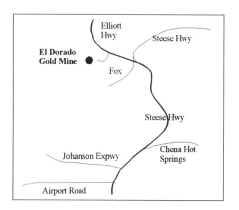

**Directions:** Mile 69 on the Steese Highway. Get specific directions when you make your reservation.

## FAIRBANKS / *Easy*

## Pan for Gold  ⁊

*The following gems or minerals may be found:*
- Gold

Gold Dredge No. 8
1755 Old Steese Highway North
Fairbanks, AK 99712
Phone: (907) 457-6058
Fax: (907) 457-8888
www.golddredgeno8.com

**Open:** Mid-May–mid-September, 9:30 A.M.–3:30 P.M., daily; tours leave every hour on the half.
**Info:** As part of the tour of Gold Dredge No. 8, pan gold just like a real Alaskan prospector. You are guaranteed to find gold during your panning experience. The water is heated, so your hands won't get too cold. For further information on the Gold Dredge tour, see the listing in Section 2.
**Features:** Pan for gold. Pans, shovels, and hands-on guidance are provided. Keep what you find; have it weighed at the "Assay Office."
**Rates:** Gold panning is provided as part of the tour. See listing under Section 2.
**Other services available:** Dining hall with miner's stew; museums and warehouse exhibits.

**Directions:** North on Steese Highway to Goldstream Road. Turn left on Goldstream Road to Old Steese Highway. Turn left on Old Steese Highway to the Gold Dredge. Map available on website.

## FAIRBANKS / *Easy*

## Pan for Gold  ⁊

*The following gems or minerals may be found:*
- Gold

Chena Hot Springs Resort
P.O. Box 58740
Fairbanks, AK 99711
Phone: (907) 451-8104;
(800) 478-4681 (U.S.)
Fax: (907) 451-8151
www.chenahotsprings.com

**Open:** Contact the resort for details of when panning is available.
**Panning fee:** Sack of pay dirt $20.00.
**Info:** Chena Hot Springs was discovered in 1905 by gold prospectors seeking to ease their painful rheumatism brought on by poor diet and grueling work. By 1912, Chena Hot Springs had become the premier resort of Interior Alaska, a mere 1- to 3-week trip by stagecoach from Fairbanks. Today it is only a 75-minute drive from Fairbanks.

The hot springs are located at the center of a 40-square-mile geothermal resource area. Water from the hot springs is 156°F and must be cooled before bathers can take advantage of its invigorating properties.

**Other services available:** Resort, lodge, and cabins; hiking trails; horseback riding; viewing northern lights; viewing wildlife; mountain biking, fishing, and rafting; cross-country skiing; snowmobiling; sleigh rides; snow coach tours; dog mushing; tent sites; RV parking; picnic sites.

**Directions:** From Fairbanks, take Steese Highway north to Chena Hot Springs Road. Follow Chena Hot Springs Road to the resort.

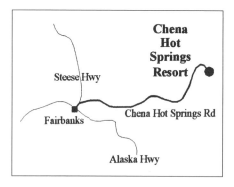

## GIRDWOOD / *Native • Easy to Moderate*

## Pan for Gold *T*

*The following gems or minerals may be found:*

- Gold

Crow Creek Mine
Cynthia Toohey and Sean Toohey
P.O. Box 113
Girdwood, AK 99587
Phone: (907) 278-8060

**Open:** May 15–October 1.

**Info:** The Crow Creek Mine was south-central Alaska's richest gold mine and there remains much unmined material. Nuggets up to ¼ of an inch are common. Some basic equipment such as pans, sluice boxes, buckets, and shovels are available.

**Rates:** Panning, $8.00/day; metal detecting, $10.00/day; motorized equipment, (such as dredges) $10.00/day for each inch on the output nozzle.

**Other services available:** Soft drink dispenser, old mining structures.

**Directions:** Located near Girdwood; call for directions.

## MCGRATH / *Native • Easy to Moderate*

## Prospect or Dredge for Gold *T*

*The following gems or minerals may be found:*

- Gold

Moore Creek Mining, LLC
Steve Herschbach or Dudley Benesch
P.O. Box 142402
Anchorage, AK 99514
Phone: (907) 277-1741
E-mail: info@moorecreek.com
www.moorecreek.com

**Open:** By appointment only.

**Info:** Over the last two years, more than 150 nuggets weighing more than 100 ounces have been found at Moore Creek using metal detectors in the tailings. The mine has a 6-inch dredge for two or more people to use, three 4-inch dredges,

three highbankers, and a 2½-inch dredge for smaller creeks. Several metal detectors are also available, or you can bring your own. You keep all the gold you find.
**Rates:** Week long stay is $1995.00. In addition, you will have to pay for airfare from Anchorage to McGrath, and also for a night's stay in McGrath. The fee covers a deluxe tent camp, food, cot with full mosquito net, shower, toilet, dredge, and fuel.
**Directions:** Get directions when you make your reservation.

## NOME / *Native • Easy to Moderate*

## Pan for Gold  *T*

*The following gems or minerals may be found:*
- Gold

Nome Beaches
Nome Convention and Visitor's Bureau
P.O. Box 240 H-P
Nome, AK 99762
Phone: (907) 443-6624
Fax: (907) 443-5832
E-mail: tourinfo@ci.nome.ak.us

**Open:** Daylight hours.
**Info:** A 40-mile stretch of beach along Norton Sound can be panned or sluiced for gold. In addition, panning is allowed along a small section of Nome Creek.
**Rates:** Free.

**Other services available:** Camping is allowed on the beach.
**Directions:** On the coast of Norton Sound, near Nome. Contact the Visitor's Bureau for more information.

## TALKEETNA / *Native • Easy to Moderate*

## Prospect for Gold  *T*

*The following gems or minerals may be found:*
- Gold

Clark/Wiltz Mining
Doug Clark
P.O. Box 586
Talkeetna, AK 99676
Phone: (907) 733-2488
E-mail: ganescreek@yahoo.com

**Open:** June–September by reservation for a one-week stay.
**Info:** One-week stays (Sunday morning to the following Saturday morning) at a camp in the Ophir mining district, roughly 45 km north of McGrath, AK. The district is known for nuggets, some up to more than 33 ounces in weight. Bring your metal detector and spend 6 days nugget hunting.
**Rates:** One-week stay is $2,500.00.
**Directions:** Get directions when you confirm your reservation.

## CHICKEN

### Gold Dredge Tour

The Chicken Gold Camp & Outpost
Box 70
Chicken, AK 99732
Phone: (907) 235-6396

Winter: Chicken Gold Camp & Outpost
4481 W. Hill Road
Homer, AK 99603
www.chickengold.com

**Open:** Call for hours and season.

**Info:** The gold camp is built on the site of the camp established for mining Chicken Creek with the Pedro Dredge. The dredge was moved to the camp and opened to the public in 2005. It is considered to be the most complete bucket line gold dredge open to the public in Alaska. Historical gold rush equipment is on display next to the dredge. Gold panning in the tailings is also available at the camp.

**Rates:** Call for rates.

**Directions:** On Airport Road, just south of the Taylor Highway, in the center of Chicken.

## FAIRBANKS

### Mine Tour

El Dorado Gold Mine
1975 Discovery Drive
Fairbanks, AK 99701

Phone: (907) 479-6673; (866) 479-6673
Fax: (907) 479-4613
E-mail: reservations@eldoradogoldmine.com
www.eldoradogoldmine.com

**Open:** Mid-May–mid-September. Tours depart 9:45 A.M. and 3:00 P.M. daily (no morning tours on Saturday).

**Info:** Reservations and prepayment required. The tour begins with a ride on an authentic narrow-gauge railroad through the past to a working gold mine. The local miners will explain mining, past and present. You pass through a permafrost tunnel and learn of the conditions miners faced working in the Arctic terrain. You can also view a large gold nugget display. The trip takes approximately 2 hours.

**Tour fee:** Adults $29.95 (includes tour of mine), children 3–12 $19.95, children under 3 free.

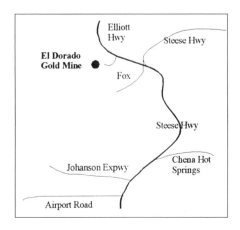

**Directions:** 9 miles north of Fairbanks on the Elliott Highway. Tours depart from the old train station at 1.3 miles on Elliott Highway, just past Fox.

## FAIRBANKS

### Mining Dredge Tour

Gold Dredge No. 8
Fairbanks, AK 99712
Phone: (907) 457-6058
Fax: (907) 457-8888
www.golddredgeno8.com

**Open:** Mid-May–mid-September. Tours start every hour on the half hour from 9:30 A.M. to 3:30 P.M. daily.
**Info:** Tour Alaska's mining history. This is Alaska's only gold dredge open to the public. See the historic dredge, bunkhouse, dining hall, and warehouse—an opportunity to see how millions of ounces of gold were recovered from the Goldstream Valley. The tour includes video and walk down Fairbanks Creek Camp, guided tour through Gold Dredge No. 8, and gold panning. The museums and warehouse exhibits can be explored at your leisure.
**Admission:** Adults $25.00, children 6–12 $12.50 (includes tour of dredge and panning). Group rates are available.

A hearty miners' stew is available from 11:00 A.M. to 3:00 P.M. in the dining hall: $9.75 for adults, $6.75 for children 6–12.
**Directions:** North on Steese Highway to Goldstream Road. Turn left on Goldstream Road to Old Steese Highway. Turn left on Old Steese Highway to the Gold Dredge.

## FAIRBANKS

### Museum

University of Alaska Museum
907 Yukon Drive
P.O. Box 756960
Fairbanks, AK 99775-6960
Phone: (907) 474-7505
Fax: (907) 474-5469
www.uaf.alaska.edu/museum/

**Open:** All year. May 15–September 15, 9:00 A.M.–7:00 P.M. September 16–May 14, 9:00 A.M.–5:00 P.M. weekdays, noon–5:00 P.M. weekends.
**Info:** The Earth Sciences collection includes excellent examples of minerals and gems from Alaska and the Pacific Rim, ore samples from Alaska and Arctic Canada, outstanding placer gold fines and nuggets, and meteorites.

A series of plate tectonic maps in the southeast gallery shows the reconstruction of Alaska's geologic history.

There is an outdoor exhibit of a mining stamp mill.
**Admission:** Adults $10.00, seniors $9.00, youth (13–18) $5.00, children under 6 free.
**Other services available:** Museum store.
**Directions:** The museum is located at 970 Yukon Drive on the University of Alaska–Fairbanks campus.

## JUNEAU

## Mine Tour 🏛

Alaska Gastineau Mill and Gold Mine
Princess Tours
151 Mill Street
Juneau, AK
Phone: (907) 463-3900
E-mail: ptoursjnu@aol.com

**Open:** June 1–October by reservation.
**Info:** Tour an old hard-rock gold mine,
watch a mining demonstration in one of
the mine tunnels. Pan for gold in the
mine tailings.
**Admission:** Adults $59.00, children
under 13 $30.00.
**Directions:** Tour buses take visitors to
the mine for the tour. Call for specific
directions when making reservations.

## JUNEAU

## Museum 🏛

Juneau-Douglas City Museum
155 S. Seward
Juneau, AK 99801
Phone: (907) 586-3572

**Open:** May 16–September 23, Monday–Friday, 9:00 A.M.–5:00 P.M.; Saturday–Sunday, 10:00 A.M.–5:00 P.M.;
October–mid-May, Tuesday–Saturday,
noon– 4:00 P.M.
**Info:** Presents the history of gold mining
in the Juneau area.
**Admission:** Summer: adults $4.00, chil-

dren under 19 free. Winter: Free.
**Directions:** At the corner of 4th and
Main Street in Juneau.

## NOME

## Museum 🏛

The Carrie N. McLain Memorial
Museum
P.O. Box 53
Nome, AK 99762
Phone: (907) 443-6630
E-mail: museum@ci.nome.ak.us

**Open:** Call for hours.
**Info:** History of gold mining in the
Nome area.
**Rates**: Call for rates.
**Directions:** On Front Street in Nome.

## WASILLA

## Mine Tour 🏛

Independence Mine State Historical
Park
Mat-Su/CB Area Park Office
HC 32 Box 6706
Wasilla, AK 99654
Phone: (907) 745-3975 or (summers
only) (907) 745-2827
www.dnr.state.ak.us/parks/units/
indmine.htm

**Open:** Summer, starting at the beginning
of June. Visitor Center hours: 10:00 A.M.–
7:00 P.M. Guided tours are offered at
1:00 P.M. and 3:00 P.M. 7days/week, with

an additional tour at 4:30 P.M. on weekends and holidays.

**Info:** The Independence Mine began as two separate mines that were combined in a single operation in the 1930s becoming the largest gold producer in the Willow Creek Mining District.

**Rates:** A parking fee of $5.00 is charged when entering the park. An additional fee is charged for the guided tour; contact the visitor center.

**Other services available:** Gold panning may be conducted in the park. See the entry for Hatcher Pass Public Use Area under State of Alaska in the section on fee dig sites.

**Directions:** Call for directions.

---

## SECTION 3: Special Events and Tourist Information

## TOURIST INFORMATION

### Field Trips

Chugach Gem & Mineral Society
Box 92027
Anchorage, AK 99509-2027
Phone: (907) 566-3403
E-mail: contact@chugachgms.org
www.chugachgms.org

**Info:** If you're visiting Alaska, contact the Chugach Gem & Mineral Society about field trips. If you are from out of town, you can subscribe to their monthly newsletter "Alaska Pebble Patter" for $10.00. The newsletter includes information on local and international field trips as well as interesting and relevant articles.

**Directions:** Contact the society for directions.

### State Tourist Agency

Alaska Travel Industry Association
2600 Cordova Street, Suite 201
Anchorage, AK 99503
www.travelalaska.com

Fairbanks Convention & Visitors Bureau
550 First Avenue
Fairbanks, AK 99701
Phone: (800) 327-5774; (907) 457-3282
www.explorefairbanks.com

# IDAHO

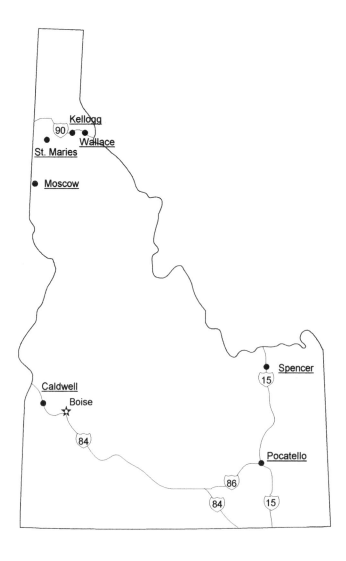

**State Gemstone:** Star Garnet (1967)

**MOSCOW /** *Native* • *Moderate to Difficult*

## Licensed Guide for Star Garnet Digging *T*

*The following gems or minerals may be found:*

▪ **Star Garnets**

3-D's Panhandle Gems and Garnet Queen Mine
Louise Darby
P.O. Box 9082
Moscow, ID 83843
Phone: (208) 882-9496

**Open:** Memorial Day weekend–Labor Day, 9:00 A.M.–5:00 P.M. Closed Wednesdays and Thursdays. Call for open sign-up dates.

All trips must be booked in advance; 30 days advance notice recommended; prepaid reservation required.

**Info:** Licensed guide service to garnet-digging activities on land in Idaho Panhandle National Forest. Idaho is one of only two locations in the world where star garnets can be found. The garnet area is located in the east and west forks of 281 draw. There is a ¾-mile walk uphill to get to the area. The east fork trip is not recommended if you have mobility problems, since the slope is very steep.

All equipment and instruction are furnished. Visitors learn where to look for star garnets, how they were formed, and how to tell a star garnet from a facet-grade garnet. Bring your own lunch, drink, and container for your garnets, and transportation to the site. Old clothes, tennis shoes or lace boots, and a change of clothing from the waist down are recommended; rubber boots are not, since they are slippery when wet.

**Fee:** $65.00 per adult, $50.00 per child 13 and under. Fee includes $10.00 National Forest Service fee and $5.00 user fee, as well as Idaho sales tax. Private trips are also available for groups of 5 or more.

**Other services available:** Wholesale and retail outlet specializing in Idaho star garnet, custom jewelry design, polishing, casting, cutting, and repairs. You can have your garnet cut and polished at the lapidary shop.

---

Idaho's nickname is the Gem State. Although much of Idaho's wealth of gems and minerals is in remote areas, to be searched only by the hardiest of rockhounds, there are some fee dig mines available. One of them is in an area that is one of only two locations in the world where star garnets can be found. The other is a location for collecting fire opals.

**Directions:** By appointment only. To the shop (1026 Juliene Way): East on Highway 8, turn right at milepost marker No. 7. Turn left and stop at the second place on the left.

## SPENCER / *Native • Easy to Difficult*

### Dig Your Own  𝑇
*The following gems or minerals may be found:*

- Precious opal

Spencer Opal Mine
HC 62, Box 2060
Spencer, ID 83446
Phone: (208) 374-5476 (May–September)
P.O. Box 521
Salome, AZ 85348
Phone: (928) 859-3752 (October–April)

**Open:** Mine shop is open 7 days/week, May–October. Fee dig at mine holiday weekends; vary each year, call for dates. Groups of 20 or more can fee dig with prior reservations.

**Info:** Dig your own opal at a "mini-mine" at the headquarters shop in a large stockpile of mine run ore. Public digging is allowed at the mine on holiday weekends. Groups may be allowed at the mine with a minimum of 2 weeks' advance registration.

The primary formation of the mine is a rhyolite and obsidian flow full of gas pockets. The opal solution, or silica, was a secondary deposit carried by geyser activity. As a result of several eruptions over time, the opal lies in layers. Most of

Star Garnets

rough gem

gem after shaping and polishing

the layers are thin, resulting in what has been said to be some of the most beautiful triplet opal in the world. Occasionally the layer will be thick enough for cutting a solid opal—a bonus for the finder.

Digging at the actual mine involves breaking rock. A rock hammer and sledgehammer are needed. Bring a spray bottle with water to clean the rock and look for color in the opal. Safety precautions for breaking rock should be followed. Wear safety glasses. Sunscreen and a sun-hat are recommended, as are long pants and hard-sided shoes or boots.

**Admission:** For "mini-mine": Adults $5.00 includes 1 pound of rock; $5.00 per pound of additional rock collected. For mine: $35.00, dig up to 5 pounds; $6.00 per pound of additional rock.

**Other services available:** The shop carries a full line of opal cutting supplies, as well as rough and finished stones and jewelry.

**Directions:** Spencer is located on I-15 in southeastern Idaho, 63 miles north of Idaho Falls, 30 miles south of Dillon,

Montana, and 70 miles west of Yellow-stone National Park. The headquarters shop is located at the north end of Main Street in Spencer, at the gas station and Opal Country Cafe.

## ST. MARIES / *Native • Moderate to Difficult*

### Dig and Wash Gravel  *T*

*The following gems or minerals may be found:*

▪ **Star garnets, garnets**

Emerald Creek Garnet Area
St. Joe Ranger District
P.O. Box 407
St. Maries, Idaho 83861
Phone: (208) 245-2531
Fax: (208) 245-6052
www.fs.fed.us/ipnf/rec/activities/garnets/

**Open:** Memorial Day through Labor Day, Friday–Tuesday.

**Info:** Northern Idaho and India are the two places in the world where star garnets are found. The 12-sided (dodecahedron) crystals range from sand-particle size to golf-ball size or larger, and are often found with four- or six-ray stars. Gem-quality faceting material is also found.

A permit is required for anyone digging, screening, or washing gravel. A permit allows you to dig in a designated area only. Up to 5 pounds of garnets may be taken under a daily permit. If you want to remove more garnets during the same day, you can buy another daily permit for an additional 5 pounds or fraction thereof. The limit is 6 permits or 30 pounds of garnet per year.

**Daily Permit Fee:** Adults $10.00, children under 14 $5.00.

Assistance provided to garnet diggers; bring your own tools (some tools available for rent).

**Other services available:** Restrooms; displays; pets are allowed on a leash.

**Nearby accommodations:** Emerald Creek Campground is 4 miles east. Campground fee is $6.00/night. This is also the location of the nearest safe drinking water. Nearest motels are in St. Marie (30 miles). Clarkia Bunkhouse Kitchen (208-245-1134) has rooms with shared showers. Food, gas, and other supplies are available in Clarkia (6 miles), Fernwood (12 miles), and Emida (25 miles). Laundromats are in Fernwood and St. Maries.

**Directions:** From St. Maries, follow Highway 3 south 24 miles to Road 447. Proceed southwest 8 miles on Road 447 to the parking area. Permits, information, and the digging area are a ½-mile hike up 281 Gulch. (Carry your equipment with you.)

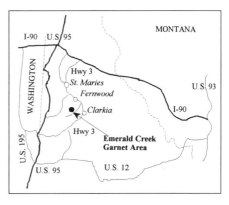

# Star Garnets

The star effect is a defect in the garnet. Also called asterism, it results from minute needles of rutile (titanium dioxide), which are found in the structure of the garnet. When light is focused on the garnet, the needles reflect it back onto the surface, causing the star. If the needles are facing in two directions, the result is a four-ray star; if the needles are facing in three directions, the result is a six-ray star. While four-ray stars are found in Idaho and in India, six-ray star garnets have been found only in Idaho.

# Digging for Star Garnets

To find star garnets, you have to dig from 1–10 feet deep. Garnets are generally found in alluvial deposits of gravel and sand just above bedrock, or in mica schist parent material.

**Equipment needed:**

- Rubber boots, waders, or old tennis shoes
- Change of clothes—garnet digging is wet, muddy work
- Standard shovel
- Bucket for bailing water
- Container for garnets—a 1-pound coffee can will hold 5 pounds of garnets
- Screen box for washing gravel

## SECTION 2: Museums and Mine Tours

### BOISE

## Museum

Museum of Mining and Geology
2455 Old Penitentiary Road
Boise, ID 83712
Phone: (208) 368-9876
E-mail: idahorox@yahoo.com

**Open:** Summer, Friday–Sunday, noon–5:00 P.M. Call for specific information.
**Info:** Offers programs and exhibits on geology and mining.
**Admission:** Free; donations appreciated.
**Directions:** Located next to the Old Penitentiary in the Historical District.

## CALDWELL

## Museum

The Glen L. and Ruth M. Evans Gem and Mineral Collection
Orma J. Smith Museum of Natural History
Alberton College of Idaho
2112 Cleveland Boulevard
Caldwell, ID 83605
Phone: (208) 459-5211
www.albertson.edu

**Open:** When college is in session, by appointment only.
**Info:** Glen and Ruth Evans presented the College of Idaho with a spectacular collection, which includes 52 glass-enclosed cases in two rooms containing Brazilian and Mexican agate, Biggs jasper, variscite, Lake Superior agate, tiger eye, Bruneau jasper, Owyhee jasper, and many other gemstones. Two revolving cases contain over 2,000 cabochons, or "cabs," made from all varieties of materials, some no longer available. Spheres of all sizes and materials number in the hundreds. Also included are carved jade from Taiwan, corals from the Pacific islands, fluorescent minerals, and native gold and silver in various forms from Idaho mines. One display contains many mineral crystals, unpolished, just as they occur in nature. The collection contains gems from all sectors of the US and from many countries. Ruth Evans faceted, cut, and polished many of the specimens. Most items in the collection are descriptively labeled.

The collection is located on the main floor of the William Judson Boone Hall (Science Center).
**Admission:** Small fee.
**Directions:** On the college campus in Caldwell, Idaho.

## KELLOGG

## Mine Tour

Crystal Gold Mine
Silver Valley Road
Kellogg, ID 83837
Phone: (208) 783-4653

**Open:** Summer, 9:00 A.M.–6:00 P.M. seven days/week. Winter, October–April, 10:00 A.M.–4:00 P.M. December–February, Saturdays and Sundays only.
**Info:** Tour an underground gold mine originally dug in 1879–1882.
**Admission:** Adults $10.00, seniors $9.00, children 4–16 $7.50, family rate (5 people) $36.00.
**Directions:** From I-90, take exit 54 to the Miner's Memorial on the north side of the interstate, then turn left (west) on Silver Valley Road, and drive 2 miles to the mine.

## KELLOGG

## Museum

Staff House Museum
Shoshone County Mining & Smelting Museum, Inc.
820 McKinley Avenue
Kellogg, ID 83837
Phone: (208) 786-4141

**Open:** May–September open daily, 10:00 A.M.–5:00 P.M.

**Info:** Museum has a 3-dimensional model of the Bunker Hill Mining and Smelting Company, as well as displays of rocks, minerals, and mining equipment.

**Rates:** Adults $4.00, seniors $3.00, children 6–18 $1.00, children under 6 free.

**Directions:** Call for directions

## POCATELLA

### Museum

Idaho Museum of Natural History
Idaho State University Campus
Campus Box 8096
5th & Dillon Street
ISU Building 12, Room 205C
Pocatello, ID 83209
Phone: (208) 236-3317
E-mail: store@imnh.isu.edu
http://imnh.isu.edu

**Open:** Tuesday–Saturday, 10:00 A.M.–5:00 P.M.

Closed Sundays, Mondays, and holidays.

**Info:** Displays of specimens from Idaho and the Intermountain West.

**Directions:** On the Idaho State University campus. Call for specific directions.

## WALLACE

### Mine Tour

Sierra Silver Mine Tour
420 5th Street
Wallace, ID 83873
Phone: (208) 752-5151
E-mail: silverminetour@imbris.com

**Open:** Daily, May–September. Tours every 30 minutes beginning at 9:00 A.M.

**Info:** Tour an underground silver mine, and learn historic and modern mining techniques. The mine is cool, so bring a light jacket.

**Admission:** Adults $9.50, seniors $8.50, children 4–16 $7.50.

**Directions:** In historic Wallace, ID. Call for specific directions.

---

## SECTION 3: Special Events and Tourist Information

## TOURIST INFORMATION

### State Tourist Agency

Division of Tourism Development
700 W. State Street
P.O. Box 83720
Boise, ID 83720-0093

Phone: (208) 334-2470
Fax: (208) 334-2631
www.visitid.org

# IOWA

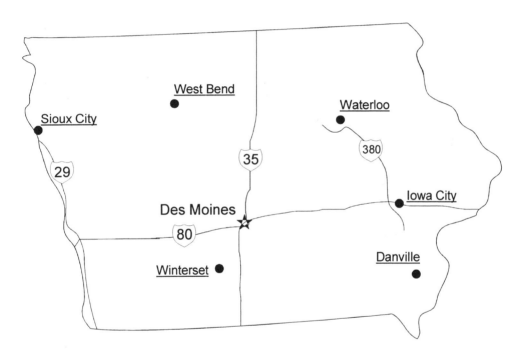

West Bend

Waterloo

Sioux City

35

380

29

Iowa City

Des Moines

80

Danville

Winterset

**State Stone/Rock:** Geode

No information available.

## DANVILLE

### Museum

Geode State Park
3249 Racine Avenue
Danville, IA 52623
Phone: (319) 392-4601
Fax: (319) 392-4605
E-mail: geode@dnr.state.ia.us

**Open:** All year round, weather permitting, 4 A.M.–10:30 P.M.; 7 days a week.

**Info:** The park is named for the geode stones which rockhounds hunt in this area. A display of geodes with a variety

of mysterious crystal formations can be found at the park office.

**Note:** *It is illegal to remove geodes from the state park.*

Not far across the state line in Missouri is a fee dig location for geodes. See the listing under Alexandria, Missouri.

**Admission:** Call for rates.

**Directions:** Geode State Park can be reached from U.S. 34, which goes between Burlington and Mt. Pleasant. Take County Highway J20 from U.S. 34 to get to the park.

## IOWA CITY

### Museum

The University of Iowa
Museum of Natural History
10 Macbride Hall
Iowa City, IA 52242
Phone: (319) 335-0480
www.uiowa.edu/~nathist

**Open:** Tuesday–Friday, 10:00 A.M.–3:00 P.M.; Saturday, 10:00 A.M.–5:00 P.M.;

Sunday, 1:00 P.M.–5:00 P.M.; closed Mondays and national holidays.

**Admission:** Free.

**Info:** Iowa Hall contains over 60 exhibits about the history of Iowa. Take a walk through the 5 billion-year story of the state's geology and natural history.

**Directions:** From Highway 218, take the Iowa City exit to Riverside Drive. Take Riverside Drive to Iowa Avenue. Or, from I-80, take exit 224, Dubuque Street, to Iowa Avenue. Take Iowa Avenue to the university campus. UIMNH is in MacBride Hall on the corner of Clinton and Jefferson Streets, next to the Old Capital Building.

## SIOUX CITY

## Museum

Sioux City Public Museum
2901 Jackson Street
Sioux City, IA 51104-3697
Phone: (712) 279-6174
Fax: (712) 252-5615
E-mail: scpm@sioux-city.org
www.sioux-city.org/museum

**Open:** Tuesday–Saturday, 9:00 A.M.–5:00 P.M., Sunday 1:00–5:00 P.M.

**Info:** Exhibits in mineralogy explain the various properties and characteristics of minerals as well as their chemical compatibilities and possible commercialization.

**Admission:** Free.

**Directions:** Located in Sioux City, at Jackson Street.

## WATERLOO

## Museum

Grout Museum of History and Science
503 South Street
Waterloo, IA 50701
Phone: (319) 234-6357
Fax: (319) 236-0500
www.groutmuseumdistrict.org

**Open:** Tuesday–Saturday 9:00 A.M.–5:00 P.M.; Sunday 1:00–4:30 P.M.

**Info:** The museum has two permanent cases displaying rocks and minerals in the main level of the museum. The hands-on children's space, the Discovery Zone, has Discovery Boxes featuring rocks, minerals, and fossils.

**Admission:** Adults $4.50, children 3–12 $3.00, children under 3 free.

**Directions:** On South Street between Park Avenue and West 4th, one block south of Highway 218.

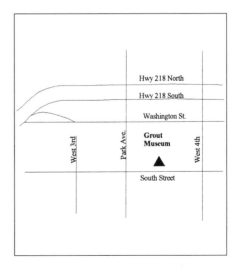

## WEST BEND

## Grotto

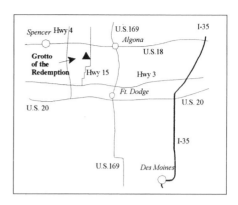

Grotto of the Redemption
300 N. Broadway
West Bend, IA 50597
Phone: (515) 887-2371
Fax: (515) 887-2372
E-mail: info@westbendgrotto.com
www.westbendgrotto.com

**Open:** Daily tours May 1–October 15 or by appointment, 10:00 A.M.–5:00 P.M. 7 days/week. Museum and grotto are open to visitors all year. Group tours by appointment. Tours can be arranged earlier in the spring and later in the fall.

**Info:** The grotto is a composite of nine separate grottos, each portraying some scene in the life of Christ. It is said to include the largest collection of precious stones and gems found anywhere in one location and is the largest grotto in the world. The grotto is said to have an estimated geological value of $2,500,000. Guided tours take approximately 1 hour and include a geological lecture in the Rock Display Studio.

The Grotto Museum includes a large display of precious and semiprecious stones from throughout the world. The grotto is flooded with spotlights for evening viewing. The church is open to the public for visits to the Christmas Chapel.

**Admission:** Suggested donation: $5.00 adults, $2.50 children.

**Other services available:** The gift store is open all year. A restaurant is available seasonally at the Grotto. The campground offers overnight camping, including showers and electrical hookups. Fees are $15.00 for campers, $10.00 for tents.

**Directions:** Take State Highway 15 south from U.S. 18 (which goes between Spencer and Algona). The grotto is 2 blocks off of Highway 15 in West Bend, approximately 8 miles from U.S. 18.

## WINTERSET

## Museum

Madison County Historical Society
815 South 2nd Avenue
Winterset, IA 50273
Phone: (515) 462-2134
E-mail:mchistory@i-rule.net
www.plantnet.com/museum.html
http://madisoncountyhistoricalsociety.com

**Open:** May 1–October 31, Monday–Saturday 11:00 A.M.–4:00 P.M., Sunday 1:00–5:00 P.M.

**Info:** An extensive collection of rocks and minerals donated by Amel Priest is displayed. Amel, who farmed 400 acres near Peru, developed an interest in collecting rocks, minerals, and fossils in response to the curiosity of his Boy Scout troop. He added to his collection by trading the fossils he found for minerals and rocks from around the world.

**Admission:** $3.00.

**Directions:** Winterset can be reached by traveling south on U.S. 169 from Exit 110 on I-80 or by traveling west on State Highway 92 from Exit 56 on I-35. 2nd Avenue is two blocks west of U.S. 169.

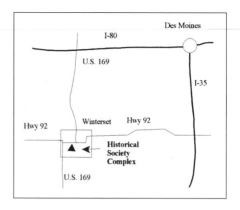

---

# SECTION 3: Special Events and Tourist Information

## TOURIST INFORMATION

### State Tourist Agency

Iowa Department of Economic Development
Iowa Tourism Office
200 E. Grand Avenue
Des Moines, IA 50309
Phone: (515) 242-4700
E-mail:info@iowalifechanging.com
www.iowalifechanging.com/contact.html

# MINNESOTA

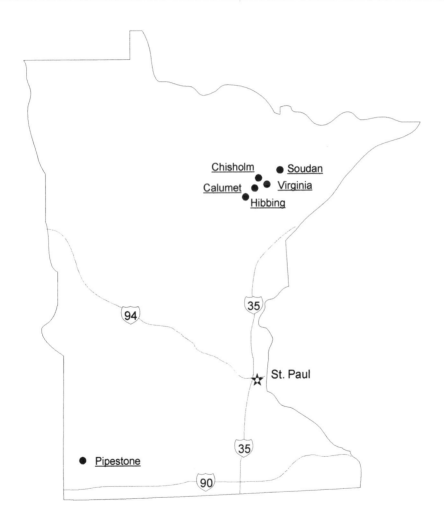

Chisholm
Calumet
Hibbing
Soudan
Virginia

94
35
St. Paul
35
90
Pipestone

**State Gemstone:** Lake Superior Agate

# SECTION 1: Fee Dig Sites and Guide Services

No information available.

# SECTION 2: Museums and Mine Tours

## CALUMET

### Mine Tour

Hill Annex Mine State Park
Minnesota Department of Natural
Resources
P.O. Box 376
Calumet, MN 55716
Phone: (218) 247-7215
Fax: (218) 247-7449
www.DNR.state.mn.us

**Open:** Memorial Day–Labor Day, 9:00
A.M.–4:00 P.M. weekdays; 9:00 A.M.–
5:00 P.M. Friday–Sunday and holidays. Bus
and mine boat tours also available. Off-
season, clubhouse museum open 10:00
A.M.–3:00 P.M., Tuesday–Friday. Group
tours available by reservation.

**Info:** On the mine tour you will descend
into Minnesota's rich history of open-pit
natural iron ore mining. See the mine's
operation area and learn about the people who worked the mine. This is a 1½-
hour tour available Friday–Sunday at

10:00 A.M. On the boat tour you will
board the pontoon boat for a trip on the
Hill Annex Mine which, for 60 years, was
one of Minnesota's most productive
open-pit natural iron ore mines. This is a
1½-hour tour available Friday–Sunday at
3:00 P.M. The Clubhouse Museum show-
cases exhibits and photos from the rich
history of the mining industry.

**Admission:** Adults $9.00, children 5–12
$6.00.

**Directions:** On U.S. 169 between Grand
Rapids and Hibbing.

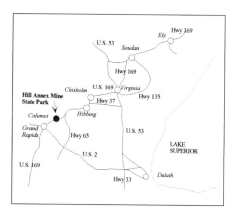

## CHISHOLM

## Mining Displays

Ironworld Discovery Center
801 SW Hwy. 169, Suite 1
Chisholm, MN 55719
Phone: (218) 254-7959; (800) 372-6437
www.ironworld.com

**Open:** May 28–September 5, 9:30 A.M.–
5:00 P.M.

**Info:** Learn about Minnesota's iron mining industry. Park includes an old-time
electric trolley, tours, climb-on equipment displays, exhibits, living history
exhibits, concerts, and ethnic meals. The
Iron Ore Miner Statue is located across
from the park, paying tribute to all the
men who worked in the early ore mines.

**Admission:** Call for rates.

**Other services available:** The Iron
Range Research Library and Archives
contain one of the largest collections of
genealogical and local history research
material in the upper Midwest. Contact
center for hours.

**Directions:** On U.S. 169 between Virginia and Hibbing.

## CHISHOLM

## Museum

The Minnesota Museum of Mining
P.O. Box 271
Chisholm, MN 55719
Phone: (218) 254-5543

**Open:** Memorial Day–Labor Day, 9:00
A.M.–5:00 P.M., Monday–Saturday; Sunday, 1:00 P.M.–5:00 P.M.

**Info:** Indoor and outdoor exhibits tell
the story of the iron mining industry in
northern Minnesota. The museum features a geological rock display, a replica
of an underground drift mine, and an old
mining town.

**Admission:** Adults $4.00, seniors $3.50,
students 5–17 $3.00.

**Directions:** In Memorial Park, at the top
of Chisholm's Main Street.

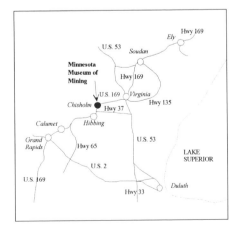

## CHISHOLM

## Mine Tour

Taconite Mine Tours
c/o Ironworld Discovery Center
801 SW Hwy. 169, Suite 1
Chisholm, MN 55716
Phone: (218) 254-3321; (800) 372-6437
www.ironworld.com

**Open:** Mid-June–mid-August, select Wednesday and Thursdays.

**Info:** Taconite is a low-grade magnetic ore that is blasted from the earth, ground to a fine powder, separated with huge magnets, pelletized, and then shipped to steel mills. The Hibbing Taconite Co. is owned by Bethlehem Steel Corporation, Cleveland-Cliffs Inc., and Stelco, Inc.

Hibbing Taconite Co. is participating with Ironworld Discovery Center to offer guided tours. Visitors will slip into steel-toed boots, put on hard hats, and embark on a 2-hour tour that will walk you through the mining process of turning iron ore into taconite pellets. The tours leave from the Ironworld Discovery Center.

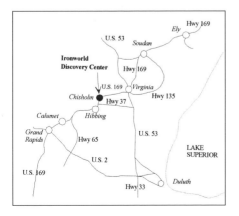

**Admission:** $5.00/person. Children must be 10 or older and accompanied by an adult.

**Directions:** On U.S. 169 between Virginia and Hibbing.

## HIBBING

## Mine Tour

Mahoning Hull-Rust Mine
Tourist Center Seniors
1202 E. Howard Street
Hibbing, MN 55746
Phone: (218) 262-4166

**Open:** May 15–mid-September, 9:00 A.M.–6:00 P.M., 7 days/week.

**Info:** The present Hull-Rust pit is reputed to be the largest open pit iron ore mine in the world. At 2,291 acres, it embraces more than 50 individual mines that were opened between 1895 and 1957. Since ore shipping began in 1895, more than 1.4 billion tons of earth have been removed from the mine. It has been called the Man-Made Grand Canyon of the North and is registered as a National Historic Site.

Attractions include mine observation stations and exterior mine exhibits.

**Admission:** Free.

**Other services available:** Walking trails; park and BBQ area.

**Directions:** On Third Avenue east in Hibbing. Take First Avenue north off US 169 to Howard Street. Take Howard Street east to Third Avenue. Take Third

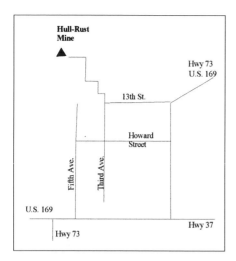

Avenue to the mine. From the north, travel south on U.S. 169 to 13th Street. Take 13th Street west to Third Avenue, then take Third Avenue north to the mine.

## PIPESTONE

## Quarry Tour 🏛

Pipestone National Monument
36 Reservation Avenue
Pipestone, MN 56164
Phone: (507) 825-5464
Fax: (507) 825-5466
www.nps.gov/pipe/

**Open:** Visitor's Center and Upper Midwest Indian Cultural Center open all year, 8:00 A.M.–5:00 P.M. (until 6:00 P.M. in summer), 7 days/week.

**Info:** Stone pipes were long known among the prehistoric peoples of North America. Digging of pipestone at this Minnesota quarry likely began in the 17th century, a time that coincided with the acquisition of metal tools from European traders. Carvers prized this durable yet relatively soft stone, which ranges in color from mottled pink to brick red. By all accounts, this location came to be the preferred source of pipestone among the Plains tribes.

Pipecarving is by no means a lost art. Carvings today are appreciated as artwork as well as for their commemoration of history. The pipestone here may be quarried only by people of Native American ancestry.

Exhibits and a slide program at the visitors' center introduce the visitor to the history and cultural significance of this area. A ¾-mile self-guiding trail tours the quarry. The Upper Midwest Indian Cultural Center demonstrates the art of pipecarving.

**Admission:** Single visitor $3.00, vehicle entrance $5.00, both valid 7 days. Annual pass available for $15.00, which covers all immediate family members.

**Directions:** Pipestone National Monument is located at the junction of U.S. 75 and State Highway 30.

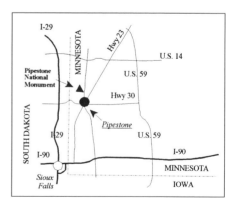

For information on other Native American stone quarries, see listings in Newark, DE: jasper quarries (Vol. 4); Calumet and Copper Harbor, MI: copper (Vol. 4); Hopewell, OH: flint quarries (Vol. 4); and Fritch, TX: flint quarries (Vol. 2).

## SOUDAN

## Mine Tour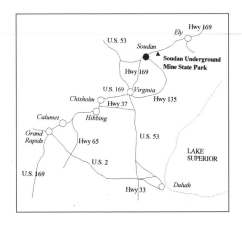

Soudan Underground Mine State Park
Minnesota Department of Natural
Resources
P.O. Box 335
Soudan, MN 55782
Phone: (218) 753-2245
E-mail: soudanmine@dnr.state.mn.us
www.dnr.state.mn.us/state_parks/soudan_
underground_mine

**Open:** Daily public tours 10:00 A.M.–4:00 P.M. May 26–end of September. After that, call for schedule. Tours run on the hour. High energy Physics Tours also available.

**Info:** The Soudan Mine was Minnesota's first underground mine and is its deepest. The tour includes a 3-minute 2,400-foot elevator ride down to the 27th level ($\frac{1}{2}$ mile underground), an electric train ride through a tunnel $\frac{3}{4}$ mile long, and a tour of the last and deepest area mined. A self-guided surface tour includes access to the ore crusher, the drill shop, and the head frame.

*Note:* The temperature of the mine is a constant 50°F; jackets and comfortable walking shoes are recommended.

**Admission:** Mine tour—adults $9.00, children 5–12 $6.00. Under 5 free. Vehicles entering the state park must have a Minnesota State park pass; which is $7.00 a day.

**Other services available:** Picnic area, hiking trails, snowmobile trails.

**Directions:** $\frac{1}{2}$ mile north from Highway 169 along the shore of Lake Vermillion.

## VIRGINIA

## Mine View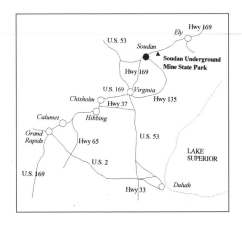

Mineview in the Sky
Laurentian Chamber of Commerce
403 1st Street N.
Virginia, MN 55792
Phone: (218) 741-2717
http://chamber.virginiamn.com

**Open:** May–October, 7 days/week.
**Info:** Mineview in the Sky overlooks the Rouchleau Mine and Rouchleau Group

of Mines, an expanse of open-pit mines that stretches nearly 3 miles in length and is a half mile wide. At its deepest point the mine is 450 feet deep. This group of mines has produced more than 300,000,000 gross tons of iron ore. The mines were originally claimed by the Merritt brothers in the late 1800s. John D. Rockefeller ultimately acquired the Merritt holdings, and eventually the properties were transferred to the United States Steel Corp., which continues to hold an interest in the operation. The overlook was originally built as a vantage point for the pit supervisors to be able to view the entire operation; today, visitors can do the same.

**Admission:** Free.

**Directions:** East side of Highway 53, at the south end of Virginia.

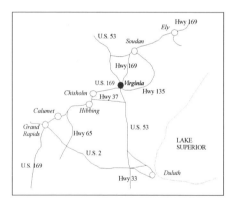

## VIRGINIA

## Mine Views

Mine Views
c/o Iron Trail Convention & Visitors Bureau
403 North 1st Street
Virginia, MN 55792
Phone: (218) 749-8161; (800) 777-8497
E-mail: info@irontrail.org

**Info:** Many mine views are available in the area. Check with the Iron Trail Convention and Visitors Bureau for information and directions. The following are some of these mine views:

### Mountain Iron Mine View
Open mid-May–October
Two sites in Mountain Iron provide views of the Minntac ore-taconite operations of U.S. Steel. One is located at the north end of Mountain Avenue; the second (called the Wacootah) is located on Highway 102.

### Leonidas Overlook
Open mid-May–October
This overlook provides a spectacular panorama of the Eveleth Taconite Operations and the Minntac Mine. Located 1 mile west of Eveleth on County Highway 101.

### Oldtown-Finntown Mine View
Open mid-May–September
Located in Virginia, this overlook offers a view of the Rocheleau Mine Group, reported to be the deepest mine in the area.

# SECTION 3: Special Events and Tourist Information

## TOURIST INFORMATION

### State Tourist Agency

Explore Minnesota Tourism
121 Seventh Place East
Metro Square, Suite 100
St. Paul, MN 55101
Phone: (800) TOURISM; (868-7476)
E-mail: explore@state.mn.us
www.exploreminnesota.com

### Minnesota State Parks

A vehicle permit ($7.00/day; $25.00/ year) is required to enter and can be purchased at any park. Normal state park operating hours are 8:00 A.M.–10:00 P.M. For more information, call (866) 857-2757 or visit www.stayatmnparks.com.

### Iron Trail Region

The Iron Trail region is set among the forests and lakes of northeastern Minnesota. The iron ore from the Mesabi range fed the nation's steel mills for more than half a century. Immigrants from more than 40 countries came to work in the mines and left behind colorful traditions, which continue today.

# MONTANA

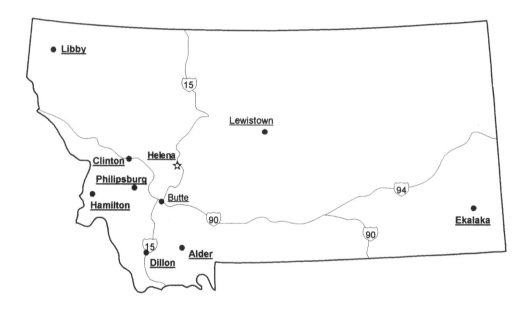

**State Stone/Rock:** Sapphire and Agate (1969)

## ALDER / *Native • Easy*

# Screen for Garnets *T*

*The following gems or minerals may be found:*

▪ Garnets of varying colors, gold, sapphires

Red Rock Mine and Garnet Gallery
Steven Cox
Box 173
Alder, MT 59710
Phone: (406) 842-5378

**Open:** May 1–October 1, 9:00 A.M.– 6:00 P.M. Monday–Saturday, noon–5:00 P.M. Sundays. Please call ahead after October 1.

**Info:** Screen for garnets in concentrated gravel left over from a pond created by gold dredging. The garnets range in color from light pink to a deep blood red. Some are of gem quality. You may also find low-grade rubies. The mine supplies screen, water, pick, and shovel. You should bring gloves and sturdy shoes. For day digs, plan to bring a shade hat, gloves, sturdy shoes,

lunch, and liquids.

**Admission:** Free, bucket $12.00, three buckets $30.00, sample bag $3.00, day digging in gravel pit $24.00 per adult for full day.

Also available are Montana gold, and Montana sapphire gravel, from other mines.

**Other services available:** Rock shop with gems, jewelry, rocks, and minerals; primitive bathrooms; picnic area; KOA campground with full facilities 1 mile west of mine.

**Directions:** 3 miles east of Alder on State Highway 287, between Alder and Ennis.

## CLINTON / *Native • Moderate to Difficult*

# Sapphire Mining Pack Trip *T*

*The following gems or minerals may be found:*

▪ Sapphires of every color in the rainbow

L◊E Guest Ranch Outfitters
Dan or Retta Ekstrom
2421 Bonita R/S Road
Clinton, MT 59825
Phone: (406) 825-6295;
(888) PAK-TRIP (725-8747)

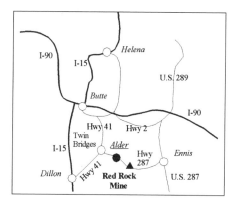

E-mail: info@ldiamonde.com
www.ldiamonde.com

**Open:** End of June–mid-September.

**Info:** Travel by horseback approximately 11 miles from the trail head. The pack trip up to the mine includes breathtaking scenery, crossing mountain streams, and encountering wildlife. The Sapphire Camp is at a proven, registered claim, located in a high mountain meadow, with a spring-fed creek running through it. After mining during the day, enjoy a delicious camp-cooked meal, then relax around the campfire and discuss your finds. Accommodations are in 9' x 9' summer tents, with foam mattresses and an outdoor shower.

**Rates:** $250.00/day per person; 4-day minimum; 30% deposit required.

**Other services available:** Trout fishing; swimming; hunting; nature photography or trail riding.

**Directions:** The L◇E Ranch is located just off I-90, 25 miles east of Missoula and 85 miles west of Butte.

**DILLON /** *Native • Moderate to Difficult*

## Dig for Quartz and Amethyst Crystals *T*

*The following gems or minerals may be found:*

• Quartz crystals, and amethyst

*Crystal Park Recreational Mineral Collecting Area*
for information:
Recreational Program Leader

Dillon Ranger District
Beaverhead-Deerlodge National Forest
420 Barrett Street
Dillon, MT 59725
Phone: (406) 683-3900
E-mail: gash@fs.fed.us

**Open:** May 15–October 30, daylight hours.

**Info:** About 30 acres of the 200 acres set aside for crystal digging are currently open. The digging area is a short walk from the paved parking area. The facilities are designed to be universally accessible. You must provide your own equipment and protective clothing.

Even in the hottest part of summer, a rain or snow shower can occur on any day at this high elevation. Also, bring a hand trowel, gardener's hand cultivator, gloves, a screen box with ¼" mesh, pack, sturdy shoes, hat, sunscreen, jacket, and insect repellent.

*Note:* Contact the U.S. Forest Service for digging tips and Crystal Park rules. Safe digging practices must be followed! Although digging is easy, because the decomposed granite is like coarse sand, it will cave in easily, quickly burying and suffocating anyone trapped under it. Be sure to follow the rules for safe digging: do not dig tunnels or deep steep-walled pits, or leave overhanging banks.

**Rates:** $6.00/car.

**Other services provided:** Three picnic areas with grills and toilets; a hand-operated water well; a paved walking trail with benches and an overlook; U.S. Forest Service campgrounds to the north and

south of the park along the scenic byway.
**Directions:** From Butte, drive 3½ miles west on I-90 to the I-15 south exit. Drive 17 miles south on I-15 to the Divide exit. From Divide, travel 11 miles west on Highway 43 to Wise River. Just past Wise River, turn south on the Pioneer Mountains Scenic Byway and drive about 25 miles to Crystal Park. The roads are paved all the way.

From Dillon, drive 2½ miles south on I-15 to the Highway 278 exit, then 22 miles west on Highway 278 to the Pioneer Mountains Scenic Byway. Turn north at this intersection onto the Byway, and drive about 17 miles up the Grasshopper Creek Valley to Crystal Park. The Byway is gravel from Highway 278 to a mile south of Crystal Park.

## HAMILTON / *Native • Moderate*

## Search for Sapphires  𝛵

*The following gems or minerals may be found:*

▪ Sapphires

Sapphire Studios
140 Aspen Grove Lane
Hamilton, MT 59840
Phone: (406) 363-6650
E-mail: gems@sapphiremining.com
www.sapphiremining.com

**Open:** Memorial Day–October, Wednesday–Saturday, noon–5:00 P.M.
**Info:** Purchase bags of ore and wash on-site, search for sapphires.
**Rates:** Free admission; bags of sapphire

gravel $25.00.
**Other services available:** Gift shop, bags of gravel shipped, gem cutting, heat treating.
**Directions:** Call or e-mail for directions.

## HELENA / *Native • Moderate*

## Dig and Screen for Sapphires  𝛵

*The following gems or minerals may be found:*

▪ Sapphires, garnets, gold, hematite, topaz, quartz, ruby, jasper, agate, jadite, serpentine

Spokane Bar Sapphire Mine and Gold Fever Rock Shop
Russ and Deb Thompson
5360 Castles Road
Helena, MT 59602
Phone: (406) 227-8989;
(877) DIG-GEMS (344-4367)
E-mail: Deb@sapphiremine.com
www.sapphiremine.com

**Open:** All year, 9:00 A.M.–5:00 P.M. (winter hours vary), 7 days/week.
**Info:** Bring your own equipment. Recommended tools include screwdriver, whiskbroom, tweezers, gloves, garden trowel, dustpan, and/or pick.
**Admission:** Free. Screen a 3½-gallon bucket of concentrate, $50.00. Dig a single 5-gallon bucket on hill and hand wash (screen), additional $10.00.
**Other services available:** Shop sells gemstones and mineral specimens, also prospecting tools. Concentrates may be ordered by UPS.

**Directions:** From Helena, take York Road to Mile Marker 8, turn right on Hart Lane. After road makes a 90° bend, turn left on Castles Road.

## LIBBY / *Native • Easy to Moderate*

## Pan for Gold  *T*

*The following gems or minerals may be found:*

• Gold

Libby Creek Recreational Gold
Panning Area
Kootenai National Forest
506 U.S. Highway 2 W.
Libby, MT 59923
Phone: (406) 293-6211
www.fs.fed.us/r1/kootenai/

**Open:** All year, daylight hours, weather permitting.

**Info:** This is gold panning in a historical gold mining area. Only hand tools and pans are allowed. Take all trash out with you.

**Rates:** Free.

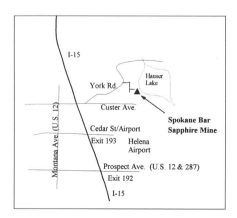

**Other services available:** Camping is allowed, with a 14-day limit. Restrooms are located at the panning area.

**Directions:** Take Highway 2 approximately 13 miles south from Libby, then turn onto Libby Creek Road and drive 10 miles to the gold panning area.

## PHILIPSBURG / *Native • Moderate*

## Search for Sapphires  *T*

*The following gems or minerals may be found:*

• Sapphires

Gem Mountain
Chris Cooney
3835 Skalkaho Road
P.O. Box 148
Philipsburg, MT 59858
Phone: (406) 859-4367; (866) 459-4367
E-mail: info@gemmtn.com
www.gemmtn.com

**Open:** Daily mid-May–mid-October, 9:00 A.M.–5:00 P.M.; later between Memorial Day and Labor Day.

**Info:** Screen and search through sapphire gravel concentrate from the mine. You can also dig mine run dirt hauled from the mine, dry-screen it, then wash the screened dirt and search for sapphires.

**Rates:** Free admission. Bucket of sapphire ore, $10.00; dig your own, $10.00. Jug of gems priced from $19.95 to $99.00.

**Other services available:** Gift shop, buckets of ore shipped to you, gem cutting, heat treating, snacks, campground that is free to customers.

# Digging for Sapphires

## Digging:

Sapphires and gold can be found in low spots and up to 3 feet above bedrock. Dig the gravel near bedrock in an open pit. After loosening the gravel, screen the material in a shaker. Throw out the larger rocks, and sift out the sand. The remaining pea gravel will fill your 5-gallon buckets. Be sure to clean your bedrock with a whiskbroom and scoop. For this step, a small pry tool or screwdriver is useful for loosening the pockets of gravel lodged in the bedrock. Sapphires and gold can rarely be seen until the gravel is washed and concentrated.

## Concentrating:

Once your buckets are filled, the screened gravel can then be concentrated in a riffled jig. The jig separates the heavier gravel. Or you may hand-wash your gravel. The hand method is time-consuming, however, and can take you up to an hour per bucket. The riffled jig will reduce your buckets of gravel down to ½ bucket of heavy concentrates in as little as 30 minutes.

Further concentrate your gravel with a hand screen. Sapphires are heavier than the surrounding material, so when you bounce or shake the screen in a tub of water, they will cluster on the bottom center of the screen. A piece of wood is then held over the top of the screenbox, and the screenbox is flipped upside down so that the gravel falls on the board without getting mixed up. If this is done properly, the sapphires will be concentrated in the center of the gravel on the board. You then pick your sapphires out of the gravel with tweezers.

You can find sapphires in every color. The natural sapphire crystal structure is hexagonal, with triangle terminations that are often flat. The most commonly found color is green-blue. Blue sapphire is the best known color. Ruby is a red sapphire and is one of the most prized.

## PHILIPSBURG / *Easy*

### Search for Sapphires  *T*

*The following gems or minerals may be found:*

- Sapphires

Sapphire Gallery
115 East Broadway
P.O. Box 2002
Philipsburg, MT 59858
Phone: (800) 525-0169
Fax: (406) 859-3631
www.sapphire-gallery.com

**Open:** All year, 10:00 A.M.–6:00 P.M. (summer), 10:00 A.M.–5:00 P.M. (winter), 6 days/week; closed Saturday.

**Info:** Visit the only all-sapphire store in the U.S., buy and wash bags of gravel in the store, and search for sapphires. When gravel is purchased and washed in the store, you are guaranteed to find a cuttable sapphire in a bag, or you will get another bag free.

The Victorian showroom, located in a Certified Historic Building, has a wide selection of sapphire jewelry.

**Fee:** Bag of gravel with one cut sapphire $25.00.

**Other services available:** Shop sells gems, fossils, and mineral specimens from around the world; goldsmithing services available; heat treating and faceting services available.

**Directions:** 115 East Broadway in Philipsburg.

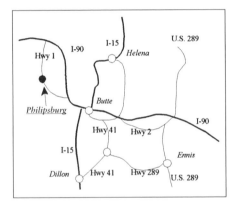

---

## SECTION 2: Museums and Mine Tours

---

## BUTTE

### Mine Tour

Anselmo Mine Yard
c/o Butte Chamber of Commerce
1000 George Street
Butte, MT 59701
Phone: (406) 723-3177; (800) 735-6814
www.butteinfo.org

**Open:** Mid-June–Labor Day 10:00 A.M.–6:00 P.M. Monday–Friday.

**Info:** The Anselmo Mine Yard and headframe are located in the Butte Historic District and constitute the best surviving example of the surface support facilities that once served the Butte mines during Butte's heyday as a first-class mining district. The visitor can tour the site and learn the history of mining in Butte. *Note:* There are no rest rooms at this location.

**Admission:** Free.

**Directions:** The mine yard is located at the intersection of Caledonia and Excelsior Streets.

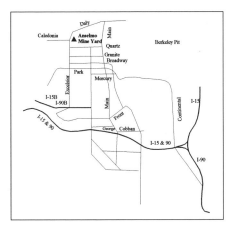

## BUTTE

## Mine View

The Berkeley Pit
c/o Butte Chamber of Commerce
1000 George Street
Butte, MT 59701
Phone: (406) 723-3177; (800) 735-6814

**Open:** Daily March–November, morning–dusk.

**Info:** The Berkeley Pit was an open-pit copper mine that started in 1955 and closed in 1982. Almost 1½ trillion tons of material were removed from this pit. Two communities and much of Butte's East Side were purchased and torn down to make way for this pit, which is 7,000 feet long, 5,600 feet wide, and 1,600 feet deep.

An observation stand can be reached by traveling Continental Drive. Coin-operated telescopes are available for close-up views. The gift shop adjacent to the stand is open in the summer and has souvenirs and information on the mine.

**Admission:** Free.

**Other services available:** Gift shop.

**Directions:** Off Continental Drive in Butte.

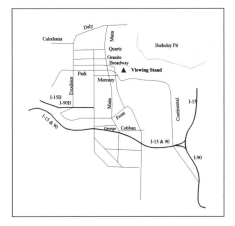

## BUTTE

## Museum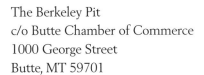

Butte-Silver Bow Visitor and
Transportation Center
1000 George Street
Butte, MT 59701
Phone: (406) 723-3177;
(800) 735-6814
Fax: (406) 723-1215
www.butteinfo.org

**Open:** Daily, May–Labor Day 8:00 A.M.–8:00 P.M., Labor Day–September 30 8:00 A.M.–5:00 P.M., October–May weekdays 9:00 A.M.–5:00 P.M.

**Info:** Displays present information about the geology and early settlement, the gold and silver area of Butte, the development of the "richest hill on earth," and the mining and smelting industry.

**Admission:** Free.

**Directions:** Just off I-15/I-90 at exit 126.

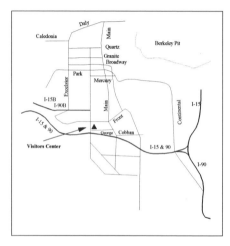

## BUTTE

## Museum

Mineral Museum
Montana Tech of the University of Montana
Butte, MT 59701
Phone: (406) 496-4414

**Open:** Memorial Day–Labor Day, daily 9:00 A.M.–6:00 P.M.; rest of the year Monday–Friday, 9:00 A.M.–4:00 P.M.; 1:00–5:00 P.M., Saturday–Sunday, May, September, and October. Guided tours can be arranged by calling.

**Info:** The museum displays more than 1,300 mineral specimens from Montana and all over the world. The collection includes a 27.8 troy ounce gold nugget and a 400-pound smoky quartz crystal found in the surrounding mountains. The fluorescent room where ordinary looking minerals radiate extraordinary vibrant shades of pink, orange, and blue when exposed to ultraviolet light is always a family favorite. The museum offers educational workshops and field trips.

**Admission:** Free.

**Directions:** The Montana Tech campus is on Park Street, which can be reached from I-15/I-90 by taking the Mountain Street exit and traveling north to Park Street.

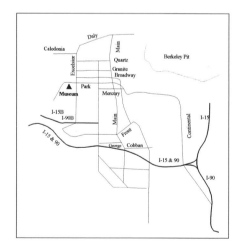

# BUTTE

## Museum

World Museum of Mining and 1899
Mining Camp
Butte, MT 59701
Phone: (406) 723-7211
www.miningmuseum.org

**Open:** Daily, April 1–October 31, 9:00
A.M.–5:30 P.M.; May 27–September 5,
9:00 A.M.–9:00 P.M.

**Info:** The World Museum of Mining and
1899 Mining Camp consists of a mining
village with over three dozen structures
located around the base of a real mining
headframe. The museum sits on 12 acres
of land surrounding the Orphan Girl
mine, which once produced silver and
zinc. Visitors can walk along the brick
streets of the mining camp or start their
tour in the hoist house. The hoist house
has mining memorabilia and historic
photos and also contains the museum
gift shop. A recent addition to the village
is a walk-through display on mining.

**Admission:** Family (2 adults and their
children 12 and under), $15; adults (over
18), $7.00; teens (13–18), $5.00; children
(5–12), $2.00; seniors over 65, $6.00.

**Other services available:** Gift shop.

**Directions:** The museum is located west
of Montana Tech. The campus is on Park
Street, which can be reached from I-15/
I-90 by taking the Mountain Street exit,
and traveling north to Park Street. Go up
the hill to the campus and past the Mar-
cus Daly statue. Just beyond the statue, a

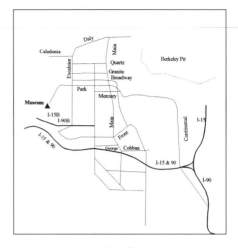

sign in the middle of the street points
straight ahead toward the museum.
Watch for the Orphan Girl mine headframe, and turn left into the museum.

# EKALAKA

## Museum

Carter County Museum
306 North Main Street
Ekalaka, MT 59324-0445
Phone: (406) 775-6886

**Open:** Daily, 9:00 A.M.–5:00 P.M.
(closed noon–1:00 P.M.) Tuesday–Friday;
1:00–5:00 P.M. Saturday and Sunday-
Winter hours: January 1–April 1 varied
hours due to the weather conditions.
Please call first.

**Info:** The Geological Department includes a fluorescent mineral display.

**Admission:** Free.

**Other services available:** Museum
store.

## Note:

For the more adventurous or advanced rockhound, the Lewistown Area Chamber of Commerce has printed materials on some rockhounding spots on Bureau of Land Management (BLM) land.

**Directions:** Ekalaka is located at the junction of Montana Highway 7 and Carter County Road 325, 35 miles south of Baker, MT.

## LEWISTOWN

## Museum

Central Montana Museum
Lewistown Area Chamber of
Commerce
408 E. Main
Lewistown, MT 59457

Phone: (406) 538-5436
Fax: (406) 538-5937
www.lewistownnews.com/discoverl
town/city.html

**Open:** Daily from Memorial Day–Labor Day (in winter, when chamber of commerce staff present), 8:00 A.M.–5:00 P.M. Monday–Friday, 10:00 A.M.–4:00 P.M. Saturday and Sunday.
**Info:** The Central Montana Museum attractions include four cases that display rocks and minerals and Yogo sapphires.
**Admission:** Donations appreciated.
**Directions:** Call for directions.

## SECTION 3: Special Events and Tourist Information

## TOURIST INFORMATION

### State Tourist Agency

Travel Montana
301 South Park
P.O. Box 200533
Helena, MT 59620-0533
Phone: (406) 841-2870; (800) VISIT MT
(847-4868)
www.visitmt.com

### State Tourist Agency

Butte Chamber of Commerce
1000 George Street
Butte, MT 59701
www.butteinfo.org

# NEBRASKA

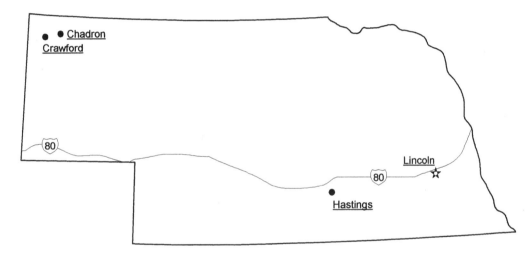

**State Gemstone:** Blue Agate
**State Stone/Rock:** Prairie Agate (1967)

# SECTION 1: Fee Dig Sites and Guide Services

No information available.

# SECTION 2: Museums and Mine Tours

## CHADRON

### Museum

Eleanor Barbour Cook Museum of
Geoscience
Chadron State College
1000 Main Street
Chadron, NE 69337
Phone: (308) 432-6377 or (800)
CHADRON
E-mail: inquire@csc.edu

**Open:** Daily, 7:30 A.M.–4:30 P.M. or by
appointment; closed major holidays and
spring break.
**Info:** Displays of rocks and minerals
from the Nebraska panhandle region,
and from Black Hills pegmatite mines;
meteorites and agates.
**Rates:** Free.
**Directions:** Call or e-mail for directions.

## CRAWFORD

### Museum

Trailside Museum
P.O. Box 462
Crawford, NE 69339
Phone: (308) 665-2929

**Open:** Daily, Memorial Day–Labor Day
9:00 A.M.–6:00 P.M.; April–May and Sep-
tember–October 10:30 A.M.–3:30 P.M.;
November–March by appointment.
**Info:** Displays of western Nebraska geology.
**Admission:** Adults $2.00, unaccompanied
children $0.50; children free if with adult.
**Directions:** The museum is located on
U.S. Route 20, in Fort Robinson State Park.

## HASTINGS

### Museum

Hastings Museum of Natural and
Cultural History
1330 North Burlington Avenue
P.O. Box 1286
Hastings, NE 68902-1286
Phone: (402) 461-4629; (800) 508-4629
E-mail: museum@alltel.net
www.hastingsmuseum.org

**Open:** Monday–Thursday 9:00 A.M.–
5:00 P.M., Friday–Saturday 9:00 A.M.–
8:00 P.M., Sunday 10:00 A.M.–6:00 P.M.
Closed Thanksgiving and Christmas Day.
**Info:** The museum has numerous specimens of minerals and rocks on display.
The museum also features a fluorescent
mineral display, as well as a display of
translucent slabs.
**Admission:** Adults $6.00, seniors $5.50,
children $4.00 (3–12).

**Other services available:** Lied Super Screen Theater, planetarium.

**Directions:** Located at 14th and Burlington (State Highway 281) in Hastings.

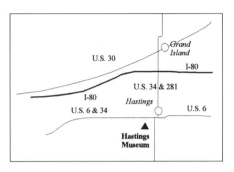

## LINCOLN

## Museum

University of Nebraska State Museum
307 Morrill Hall
Lincoln, NE 68588-0338
Phone: (402) 472-2642
www.museum.unl.edu

**Open:** Monday–Saturday 9:30 A.M.–4:30 P.M., Sundays and most holidays 1:30–4:30 P.M., closed on major holidays.

**Info:** This is the largest natural history museum in Nebraska; it has numerous specimens of minerals and rocks on display. The museum also has a fluorescent mineral display.

**Admission:** Adults $4.00, children 5–18 $2.00.

**Directions:** Exit I-80 at 27th Street and follow signs to Vine Street, then turn right. An alternate route is to take I-180 to the 14th Street exit and follow signs to the State Fair Park entrance. Go past the State Fair Park entrance to Vine Street, then turn right. Vine Street leads to 14th Street. Turn left to Morrill Hall. Limited parking during weekdays is available in front of the Hall; on weekends, additional parking is available in Lot 17c. Public parking is available within 10 minutes' walking distance from the hall.

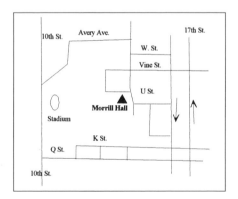

---

## SECTION 3: Special Events and Tourist Information

---

## TOURIST INFORMATION

## State Tourist Agency

Nebraska Division of Travel & Tourism
Department of Economic Development
Box 98907
Lincoln, NE 68509-8907
Phone: (877) NEBRASKA
www.visitnebraska.org

# NORTH DAKOTA

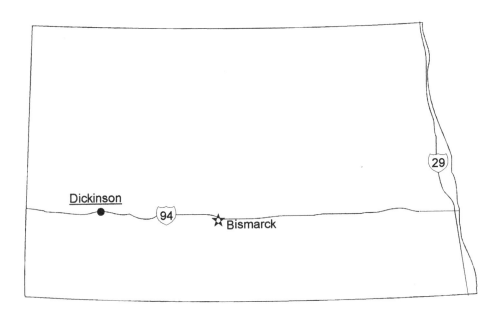

No information available.

## DICKINSON

### Museum

Dakota Dinosaur Museum
200 E. Museum Drive
Dickinson, ND 58601
Phone: (701) 225-3466
www.dakotadino.com

**Open:** Memorial Day–Labor Day 9:00
A.M.–5:00 P.M. daily. Check with museum for winter hours.

**Info:** The museum has exhibits of rocks and minerals. New exhibits include borax from California, turquoise from Arizona, and fluorescent minerals. Also on display are "aurora crystals," natural quartz crystals from Arkansas, which have been subjected to a process of plasma ionization that deposits atomically thin layers of titanium, which then interacts with the crystal structure.

**Admission:** Adults $6.00, children 3–12 $3.00. Call for group rates.

**Other services available:** Gift shop with rock and mineral specimens.

*Other local attractions in the Museum Center at Dickinson include:*
• Joachim Regional Museum: Local artifacts and displays
• Pioneer Machinery Museum
• Prairie Outpost Park: Historical buildings include house, general store, post office, Burlington Northern depot, church, rural school, pioneer stone house, chapel, Scandinavian stabbur, and coal mine entrance.

**Directions:** From I-94 take exit 61 (Route 22). Take Route 22 south to the first traffic light, and turn left on Museum Drive.

# SECTION 3: Special Events and Tourist Information

## TOURIST INFORMATION

### State Tourist Agency

North Dakota Tourism Division
Century Center
1600 E. Century Avenue, Suite 2
P.O. Box 2057
Bismark, ND 58502
Phone: (701) 328-2525;
(800) HELLO-ND (435-5663)
www.ndtourism.com

# OREGON

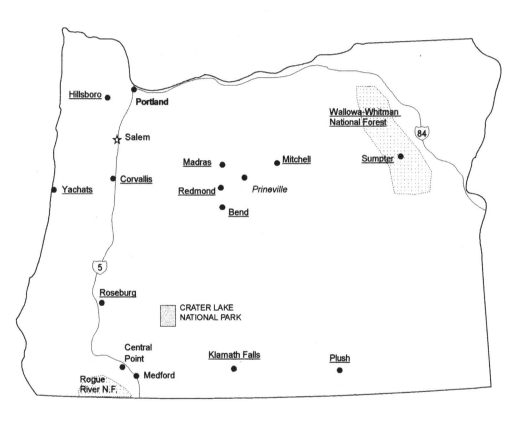

**State Gemstone:** Sunstone (1987)
**State Stone/Rock:** Thunderegg (1965)

# Rockhounding in Oregon

From the early days of the lapidary hobby in America, Oregon has played a major role. Many of Oregon's treasures are in the quartz family: thundereggs or geodes (agate or jasper), agate, picture jasper, agatized wood, and carnelian. In the state one may also find gold, obsidian, cinnabar, zeolite, and more. Not all are found at fee dig sites; at the fee dig sites listed here, one may find thundereggs, moss agate, picture jasper, ledge agate, and petrified cypress. For the more adventurous, the Chambers of Commerce in Madras and Prineville have helpful information on prospecting areas.

# Oregon Thundereggs

The Oregon state rock is the thunderegg. Thundereggs are usually found in volcanic ash and could be up to 60 million years old. They were named by the Warm Spring Indians, whose legend goes as follows:

Mt. Hood and Mt. Jefferson, two adjacent snow-capped peaks that tower over central Oregon, would at times become angry with each other. They would rob the nests of the thunderbirds and hurl the eggs at each other.

In reality, the round shape of the thundereggs is due to the fact that the agates were formed in pockets created by steam and gases in hardening volcanic flows. When sliced and polished, the interiors can contain many colors of silica materials or crystals. They are used to make jewelry and rock products. The most beautiful are found in central Oregon. The town of Prineville claims to be the "agate capital of the U.S." There are also several areas in eastern Oregon that produce specimens.

## KLAMATH FALLS / *Native • Difficult*

### Hunt for Fire Opal *T*

*The following gems of minerals may be found:*

- Fire opal

Juniper Ridge Opal Mine
5215 Sunnyside Drive
Klamath Falls, OR 97601
Phone: (541) 892-2219
E-mail: ken@juniperridgeopal.com
www.juniperridgeopal.com

**Open:** By reservation only.

**Info:** This is hard-rock mining for facet-grade fire opal. Bring eye-protection, hand tools for hard-rock mining (such as sledge hammers, chisels, rock hammers, gloves), food, and beverages. Temperatures can range from cold to hot, so layered clothing is recommended.

**Fees:** Mining fee is $175.00/person, for a 1-gallon bucket of opal. Additional fee charged if more is taken out. Opal can be high-graded before leaving.

**Directions:** Get specific directions when making your reservation.

## MADRAS / *Native • Easy to Difficult*

### Dig for Thundereggs *T*

*The following gems or minerals may be found:*

- Thundereggs, agate (ledge agate

Thunderegg

material), moss agate, jasper, polka-dot jasp-agate, rainbow agate

Richardson's Recreational Ranch
Gateway Route, Box 440
Madras, OR 97741
Phone: (541) 475-2680; (541) 475-2839; (800) 433-2680
http://richardsonrockranch.com

**Open:** Digging all year, weather permitting, all day. Office hours: 7:00 A.M.–5:00 P.M., 7 days/week.

**Info:** Digging for thundereggs requires rock picks, which are available for free day use. Digging for ledge agate requires chisels, wedges, and hard rock mining tools. Tools are available for sale at the shop, or bring your own. All diggings are easily accessible by road. Material is also available at the office.

Richardson's Recreational Ranch is a family-owned and -operated enterprise providing year-round family recreation.

It is also a working cattle ranch.

**Rates:** Call for fees.

**Other services available:** Rock shop: Buy thundereggs, moss agate, jasper, jaspagate, Oregon sunstone, rainbow agate, and other gems and minerals. Purchase rough or finished products. Also on sale are Richardson's high-speed sanders and other brands of lapidary machines and supplies.

Free campground area for rockhounds; no hookups. Free showers at shop for customers.

**Directions:** Drive 11 miles north of Madras on U.S. 97. Then turn right, and drive 3 miles to the ranch office.

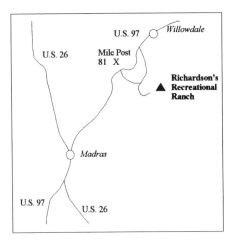

**MITCHELL /** *Native • Easy to Moderate*

## Dig for Thundereggs  *T*

*The following gems or minerals may be found:*

• Thundereggs

Lucky Strike Geodes
Leonard "Kop" Kopcinski
P.O. Box 128
Mitchell, OR 97750
Phone: (541) 462-3073
E-mail: info@luckystrikemine.com
www.luckystrikemine.com

**Open:** Mid-May–November (weather permitting) 8:00 A.M.– 5:00 P.M. Closed Tuesday and Wednesday.

**Info:** Dig your own, or select from predug material. Kop also owns another mine, the Valley View, which he may take you to upon request (weather permitting). If the weather is bad or if late snow has the mines closed, Kop has 50 tons of thundereggs in Mitchell that you can pick through. Digging for thundereggs requires rock picks which you should supply if possible. Limited assistance is available.

**Rates:** You dig: $1.00/pound.

**Other services available:** Rock shop: Buy thundereggs, moss agate, and picture jasper. Purchase rough or finished products. The shop displays a large collection of picture jasper and other gems polished or made into jewelry (not for sale).

Free primitive campground; no hookups. Spring water is available.

**Directions:** The Lucky Strike mine is located in Crook County. From Prineville, drive east on U.S. 26 for 33 miles to a point between mileposts 49 and 50. Cross the cattle guard on the left then travel 0.8 miles on Forest Road 27 to the intersection with Forest Road 2730, then 11.2 miles on Forest Road 2730 to Forest Road

# Authors' Note

Our first experience with thundereggs was at the Lucky Strike Mine owned and run by Leonard "Kop" Kopcinski. At 84, Kop is a rugged individualist, who will share with you his ideas on subjects dear to the hearts of many Westerners: private property; mining claims, and the individual's rights to them. The Lucky Strike is located in the Ochaco National Forest; the nearest town is Mitchell, Oregon. The drive up the mountain is breathtaking, and once you are at the mine, the scenery is tranquil. We parked our RV at the mine and woke up to chipmunks searching for handouts, and deer walking the path to the thunderegg mine.

Walt, Kop's sidekick, took us up to the dig in a pickup and showed us how to pull the thundereggs out of the ground with picks. They were plentiful.

Back at the mine office, Kop proceeded to show us tips on identifying good thundereggs. We shipped a hundred pounds of the beauties home (the packaging store sure appreciated our business).

Kop has a collection of some of the finest picture jasper in the world. He also has polished and unpolished pieces of picture jasper and thunderegg slabs for sale. We picked out some that had definite landscaped appearances: mountains, clouds, sunsets, and one the kids said looked like Darth Vader.

Kop plans to build a mineral museum on his property in Mitchell to display the extensive collection of minerals he has accumulated over the years.

# Cutting Thundereggs

After shipping the thundereggs home, the authors decided that they "had to have" a means to find out what was inside them. They visited their local rock shop and were able to purchase a 10" diamond saw and an arbor (used for rock polishing). This used equipment had been customized by a lapidarist and had built-in shelves and electrical connections—a real find.

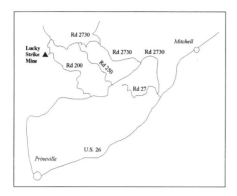

200. Follow the signs on Forest Road 200 another 2 miles to the mine. The Valley View is another 2 miles up the road.

**PLUSH /** *Native ▪ Moderate*

## Dig Your Own Sunstones  *T*

*The following gems or minerals may be found:*

▪ **Oregon sunstones**

Dust Devil Mining Co.
P.O. Box 55
Plush, OR 97637
Phone: (503) 559-2495, 559-9338, or 559-5129

Winter address:
P.O. Box 279
Cloverdale, OR 97112
Phone: (503) 965-7707
Fax: (503) 965-7706
www.dustdevilmining.com

**Open:** Daily, May–October; open later weather permitting.

**Info:** This mine has yielded large, clear, facetable sunstones in red/green bicolor, watermelon, red, and dichroic varieties. Bring beverages, snacks, clothing for hot and cool weather, shovel, screen, eye protection, sun protection, gloves, and tools for breaking rock.

**Rates:** Free admission. Pay for only the high quality or collector grade stones you take. These will be charged at 33% of the wholesale cost the mine charges for their own stones.

**Other services available:** Rock shop, pit toilets. Camping is allowed at the mine.

**Directions:** From Plush, OR, travel north on CR 3-10 (Hogback Road), which is the main road through Plush. The pavement ends 5½ miles after leaving Plush. Drive 5½ more miles, and you will come to the intersection with CR 3-11. Turn right at this intersection onto CR 3-11, travel ½ mile, then turn left at the intersection with BLM 6155. Drive 7 miles and turn left at the intersection with BLM 6115, and drive to the mine.

**PLUSH /** *Native ▪ Moderate*

## Dig Your Own Sunstones  *T*

*The following gems or minerals may be found:*

▪ **Oregon sunstones**

Spectrum Sunstone Mines
High Desert Gems & Minerals
Phone: (775) 772-7724 (Phone sometimes not in network, so keep trying.)
E-mail: tourmalineminer@aol.com
www.highdesertgemsandminerals.com

**Open:** Memorial Day–October 31, daylight hours.

**Info:** Dig Oregon sunstones at a 20-acre privately owned mining claim.

**Fees:** Free; two-day limit.

**Other services available:** Water well on-site, pit toilets are available, and camping is allowed. Housing is being constructed. Inquire about fee digging possibilities at other sunstone mines owned by High Desert Gems & Minerals.

**Directions:** From Highway 140, turn north at Adel to Plush, go through Plush, and 9.1 miles north of Plush, turn right. Travel for ½ mile, and turn left at the intersection with BLM 6155. Drive 7 miles and turn left at the intersection with BLM 6115, and drive to the mine. The Spectrum is past the Dust Devil Mine.

## ROSEBURG / *Native • Easy to Moderate*

## Pan for Gold  *T*

*The following gems or minerals may be found:*

▪ Gold

Cow Creek Recreational Area
Bureau of Land Management
777 N. Garden Valley Boulevard
Roseburg, OR 97470
Phone: (541) 440-4930
E-mail: or100mb@or.blm.gov

**Open:** Daylight hours, weather permitting.

**Info:** A 1300-foot segment of the lower stem of Cow Creek has been designated as a recreational gold panning area. The area is located in the middle of the Cow Creek Back Country Byway.

**Rates:** Free; two-day limit.

**Other services available:** Vault toilet, picnic tables.

**Directions:** On Cow Creek Road, (BLM Road 30-6-32.0), between mile 17 and mile 18.

## YACHATS / *Native*

## Find Your Own  *T*

*The following gems or minerals may be found:*

▪ **Agates, jasper**

City of Yachats Visitors Center
P.O. Box 728
Yachats, OR 97498
Phone: (541) 547-3530; (800) 929-0477
E-mail: info@yachats.org

**Info:** Stroll the beaches and collect agates and jasper. The most plentiful agate and jasper deposits are present on beaches backed by sandstone bluffs and along the shoreline, where you can see patches of gravel. The best beaches are those that have exposed basalt near them where the sea can pound on the rock to release the embedded beauties. Another good place to look is along the shore of any rocky stream or river where it crosses a beach. Often agate washed out of basalt high in the Coast Range will be carried on watercourses

# Gold Panning Sites on Federal Land

Several areas have been set aside for recreational gold panning on federal lands. These sites are considered to be easy to moderate.

**Oregon Quartzville Recreational Corridor, in the Western Cascades**

BLM
Salem District Office
1717 Fabry Road SE
Salem, OR 97306
Phone: (503) 375-5646

**Butte Falls Recreational Area,**
in southwest Oregon.

BLM
Medford District Office
3040 Biddle Road
Medford, OR 97504
Phone: (541) 770-2200

**Applegate Ranger District,** Rogue River National Forest has panning areas adjacent to four campgrounds.

Applegate Ranger District
6941 Upper Applegate Road
Jacksonville, OR 97539
Phone: (541) 899-1812

**Wallowa-Whitman National Forest**, located in northeast Oregon, has three areas set aside: the Eagle Forks Campground, the McCully Forks Campground, (which also includes Deer Creek Campground and Powder River Recreational Area), and the Antlers Guard Station.

• Wallowa-Whitman National
  Forest Supervisor
  P.O. Box 907
  Baker City, OR 97814
  Phone: (541) 523-6391

• Eagle Forks Campground
  Pine Ranger District
  Halfway, OR 97834
  Phone: (541) 742-7511

• McCully Forks Campground
  Baker Ranger District
  Baker City, OR 97814
  Phone: (541) 523-4476

• Antlers Guard Station
  Unity Ranger District
  Unity, OR 97884
  Phone: (541) 446-3351

**Rates:** All areas are free, except the Applegate Ranger District Campgrounds, where there is a $1.00 fee.

*Note:* Locations and some directions can be found by visiting www.oregongeology.com, or contacting the Oregon Department of Geology and Mineral Industries at:

800 NE Oregon Street
Portland, OR 97232
Phone: (503) 731-4100

down to the sea. Some agate beds are uncovered year round, while others are only open at unpredictable intervals. The most successful hunter is one who haunts the beaches on the outrunning tides from December through March. Stonefield Beach Wayside, 6 miles south of Yachats, is one of the best beaches for all kinds of beachcombing.

**Admission:** Free.

## CENTRAL POINT

## Museum

Crater Rock Museum
Roxy Ann Gem and Mineral Society, Inc.
2002 Scenic Avenue
Central Point, OR 97502
Phone: (541) 664-6081
www.craterrock.com

**Open:** Tuesday, Thursday, and Saturday, 10:00 A.M.–4:00 P.M.

**Info:** Founded in 1954, the museum contains excellent specimens of minerals, thundereggs, fossils, geodes, and cut and polished gemstones. The collection of minerals is arranged in a sequence useful for understanding minerals, how they are used, and their content.

A large meteorite, amber displays, and an excellent display of cut and polished sections of petrified wood, identified as to species, are on display.

The museum is owned by the Roxy Ann Gem and Mineral Society, Inc., a nonprofit organization. Programs for school students, including classroom displays, are available. The society also offers: access to the earth science library, field trips to collecting sites, and workshops on lapidary arts, faceting, jewelry design, and fabrication.

**Admission:** Free.

**Directions:** Traveling south on I-5, take Exit 35 and follow Highway 99 to Scenic Avenue. There is a highway sign for the museum. Scenic Avenue is marked by an overhead yellow caution light; turn left onto Scenic Avenue to the museum.

Traveling north on I-5, take Exit 32, turn left, and follow Pine Street through Central Point to the stoplights for Highway 99. Turn right on Highway 99 and travel for 2 miles. There is a highway sign for the museum. Scenic Avenue is marked by an overhead yellow caution light; turn left onto Scenic Avenue to the museum.

## CORVALLIS

## Museum

Department of Geosciences
104 Wilkinson Hall
Oregon State University
Corvallis, OR 97331-5506

> **Agate** results from silica filling empty gas pockets or cracks in rock, creating nodules or seams of agate. Since only limited amounts of foreign minerals are included, the resulting agate is generally pure. It ranges from clear to translucent when held up to the light. Clear agate with no color or pattern is called white agate; orangish-red agate is carnelian. Sard is clear to translucent agate with a yellow-orange to dark brown tinting.
>
> **Jasper** is an opaque stone, a variety of chert, resulting from deposits within sedimentary material. It contains a high percentage of impurities, which gives it high coloration.

Phone: (541) 737-1201
Fax: (541) 737-1200
E-mail: geo-info@geo.oregonstate.edu

**Open:** When school is open. Call for specific times.

**Info:** One of the finest mineral displays in the Pacific Northwest devoted to instruction in Earth Sciences.

**Admission:** Free.

**Directions:** In Wilkinson Hall, on the west main floor.

## HILLSBORO

## Museum

Rice Northwest Museum of Rocks & Minerals
26385 NW Groveland Drive
Hillsboro, OR 97124
Phone: (503) 647-2418
Fax: (503) 647-5207
E-mail: info@ricenwmuseum.org
www.ricenwmuseum.org

**Open:** All year, Wednesday–Sunday, 1:00 P.M.–5:00 P.M.

**Info:** Has an extensive collection of minerals, crystals, fluorescent minerals, agates, thundereggs, and some extraordinary lapidary work.

**Admission:** Adults $5.00, seniors $4.50, students $3.50, children under 6 free.

**Other services available:** Gift shop, rock pile for students to select a free specimen.

**Directions:** Off Highway 26 West, take exit 61 North, then take first turn west onto Groveland Drive, to the museum.

## REDMOND

## Point of Interest

Petersen's Rock Garden
7930 S.W. 77th Street
Redmond, OR 97756
Phone: (541) 382-5574

**Open:** All year. Summer hours: 9:00 A.M.–6:00 P.M. museum, 9:00 A.M.–7:00 P.M.

outside. Winter hours: 9:00 A.M.–4:30 P.M. museum, 9:00 A.M.–dusk outside.

**Info:** This unusual garden is the 17-year creation of Rasmur Petersen, a Danish immigrant farmer, and has 4 acres of miniature rock structures. Almost all the rocks used come from within an 85-mile radius of the gardens. Included are petrified wood, agate, jasper, thundereggs, malachite, lava, and obsidian.

The museum houses thousands of rock specimens and a fine fluorescent rock display.

**Admission:** Donation requested; adults $3.00, children 12–16 $1.50, children 6–11 $0.50.

**Other services:** Gift shops; picnic area with tables, fireplaces, and free-roaming peacocks, ducks, and chickens to help you with your lunch.

**Directions:** 2½ miles west of Highway 97 between Redmond and Bend.

## SUMPTER

### Mining Dredge Tour

Sumpter Valley Dredge State Heritage Area
Greater Sumpter Chamber of Commerce
P.O. Box 250
Sumpter, OR 97877

Phone: (541) 894-2486; (800) 551-6949
Fax: (541) 894-2445
www.triax.com/sumpter

**Hours:** 10:00 A.M.–4:00 P.M.

**Info:** View a gold dredge: the dredge that rests at the edge of Sumpter was built by the Sumpter Valley Dredge Co. in 1935. It shut down between 1942 and 1945 because of World War II, then operated under various owners until all dredging in the valley ceased in 1954. The dredge recovered more than $4.5 million during its heyday, and over $10 million in gold was recovered by dredging in Sumpter Valley alone.

**Admission:** Free.

**Other attractions:** Tour the historic gold rush towns of Sumpter and Granite.

**Directions:** Take Exit 306 on I-84, then follow State Highway 7 west to Sumpter. Off OR 7, 30 miles west of Baker City.

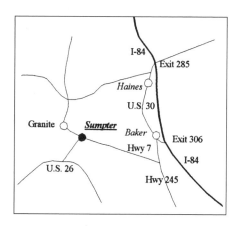

## PRINEVILLE

### Prineville Crook County Chamber of Commerce

390 NE Fairview
Prineville, OR 97754
Phone: (541) 447-6304
Fax: (541) 447-6537
pchamber@prineville.org

**Info:** Crook County, Oregon claims the title "Rockhound Capital of the World." The Chamber of Commerce provides a helpful guide to types of rocks you can expect to find in the area. Call for cost.

The Chamber of Commerce also sponsors a Rockhounds Pow-Wow in mid-June each year. Amateur rockhounds and commercial dealers bring equipment and materials to sell or trade.

## ANNUAL EVENT

### Bohemia Mining Days

Bohemia Mining Days
Cottage Grove, OR 97424
Phone: (541) 942-5064
www.bohemiaminingdays.org

**Info:** Third week in July; features Oregon State Gold Panning Championship, Western States Gold Mining Exposition, treasure hunt, concerts, demonstrations.

## TOURIST INFORMATION

### State Tourist Agency

Oregon Tourism Commission
670 Hawthorne Street SE, Suite 240
Salem, OR 97301
Phone: (800) 547-7842
www.traveloregon.com

# SOUTH DAKOTA

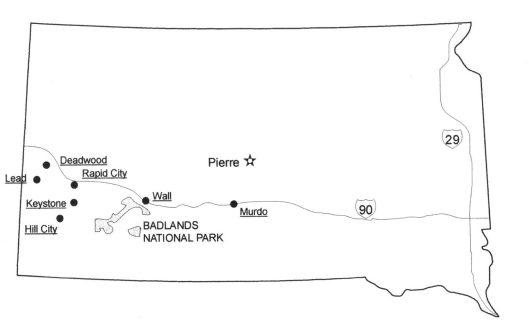

**State Gemstone:** Fairburn Agate (1966)
**State Mineral/Stone:** Rose Quartz (1966)

## DEADWOOD / *Easy*

## Pan for Gold  ⊤

*The following gems or minerals may be found:*

▪ Gold

Broken Boot Gold Mine
735 Main Street
Deadwood, SD 57732
Phone: (605) 578-9997

**Open:** Mid-May–mid-September, 8:30 A.M.–5:30 P.M., 7 days/week.
**Panning fee:** $5.00.
**Other services available:** Restrooms.
**Info:** For more information on the mine tour and the city of Deadwood, see listing in Section 2.
**Directions:** Located at the south end of Historic Deadwood, at the junction of Upper Main Street and Highway 14A.

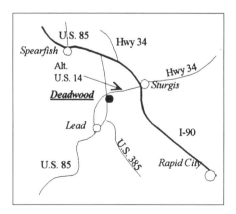

## HILL CITY / *Native ▪ Easy*

## Pan for Gold  ⊤

*The following gems or minerals may be found:*

▪ Gold

Wade's Gold Mill
P.O. Box 312
Hill City, SD 57745
Phone: (605) 574-2680
E-mail: wades@wadesgoldmill.com
www.wadesgoldmill.com

**Open:** Memorial Day–Labor Day, 9:00 A.M.–6:00 P.M.
**Info:** Learn how to pan gold. A panning lesson can be provided by an experienced gold miner which includes a sample of gold ore guaranteed to have gold. Buckets of ore from Wade's gold mine can be purchased.
**Rates:** Panning lesson, $6.00; bucket of gold ore, $3.00.
**Other services available:** Tour of the mine facilities. See Section 2.
**Directions:** Call for directions.

## KEYSTONE / *Easy*

## Pan for Gold  ⊤

*The following gems or minerals may be found:*

▪ Gold

Big Thunder Gold Mine
Box 459
604 Blair Street
Keystone, SD 57751
Phone: (605) 666-4847; (800) 314-3917
E-mail: mclainsandra@aol.com
www.bigthundergoldmine.com

**Open:** June–Labor Day 8:00 A.M.–8:00 P.M.; May, September–October 9:00 A.M.–6:00 P.M. 7 days/week.
**Admission for panning:** $4.95 with mine tour, $6.95 without tour.
**Info:** The mine is handicapped accessible.
**Other services available:** Restrooms. For more information on the mine tour, see listing in Section 2.
**Directions:** Off Highway 40.

Black Hills Mining Museum
323 West Main Street
P.O. Box 694
Lead, SD 57754
Phone: (605) 584-1605
E-mail: bhminmus@mato.com
www.mining-museum.blackhills.com

**Open:** All year. May–August 9:00 A.M.–5:00 P.M.; September–May, Monday–Friday 9:00 A.M.–4:30 P.M.
**Cost for panning:** $4.50–$5.00 in addition to museum admission.
**Info:** For more information on the museum, see listing in Section 2.
**Other services:** Simulated mine tour (see Section 2 for more information); gift shop, which sells gold panning supplies.
**Directions:** Lead is located on U.S. 85, south of I-90.

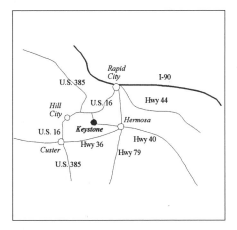

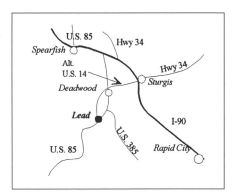

**LEAD /** *Easy*

## Pan for Gold ⟑

*The following gems or minerals may be found:*

▪ Gold

**WALL /** *Native ▪ Difficult*

## Hunt for Rocks and Minerals ⟑

*The following gems or minerals may be found:*

▪ Agates

Buffalo Gap National Grassland
Wall Ranger District
Box 425
Wall, SD 57790
Phone: (605) 279-2125
www.fs.fed.us/r2/nebraska/recreation

**Open:** Visitor Center open all year, Memorial Day–Labor Day 8:00 A.M.–5:00 P.M.; rest of the year 8:00 A.M.–4:30 P.M., Monday–Friday. Hours subject to change.

**Info:** The surface collection of rocks and minerals for personal use is allowed without a permit. The collection of these items for future barter, sale, etc., would require a permit, as would any excavation or surface disturbance.

The Buffalo Gap National Grassland map is available. This map shows the land status of different public and private lands. To request a map, call (605) 279-2125. The map can also be purchased at the Visitor Center in Wall.

**Admission:** Free.

**Directions:** Take exit 110 off I-90, travel north to South Boulevard. Turn left on South Boulevard for two blocks, then turn right on Main Street to the visitor center.

## SECTION 2: Museums and Mine Tours

### DEADWOOD

## Mine tour

Broken Boot Gold Mine
735 Main Street
Deadwood, SD 57732
Phone: (605) 578-1876
www.brokenbootgoldmine.com

**Open:** Mid-May–mid-September, 8:30 A.M.–6:30 P.M., 7 days/week.

**Info:** Step back in time to experience late 1800s gold mining. Visitors receive a souvenir share of stock in the Broken Boot Mine after the tour.

The city of Deadwood is a designated National Historic Landmark, and there are many recreation activities nearby.

**Admission:** Call for prices.

**Other services available:** Mine tour, gift shop, restrooms.

**Directions:** Located at the south end of Historic Deadwood, at the junction of Upper Main Street and Highway 14A.

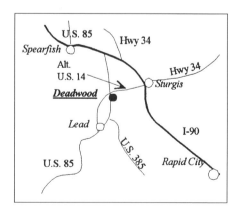

## HILL CITY

## Mine Museum and Tour

Wade's Gold Mill
P.O. Box 312
Hill City, SD 57745
Phone: (605) 574-2680
E-mail: wades@wadesgoldmill.com
www.wadesgoldmill.com

**Open:** Memorial Day–Labor Day, 9:00 A.M.–6:00 P.M.

**Info:** A guided tour includes a demonstration of mining techniques and displays of new and old mining equipment, much of which has been restored.

**Rates:** Guided tour, adults $8.00, children 6-11 $4.00. Guided tour with gold panning lesson: Adults $12.50, children 6-11 $9.00.

**Other services available:** Gold panning lessons, and gold mine ore for panning.

**Directions:** Call for directions.

## KEYSTONE

## Mine Tour

Big Thunder Gold Mine
Box 459
Keystone, SD 57751
Phone: (605) 666-4847; (800) 314-3917

**Open:** June–Labor Day 8:00 A.M.–8:00 P.M., May and September–October 9:00 A.M.–6:00 P.M., 7 days/week.

**Info:** Relive the experience of 1880s gold mining. Free samples of gold ore are given on the underground mine tour. The mine is handicapped accessible.

**Admission:** Call for tour and tour plus panning prices.

**Other services available:** Mine tour, gift shop, restrooms.

**Directions:** Off Highway 40.

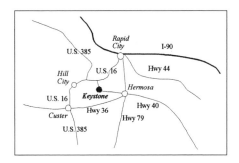

## LEAD

## Museum

Black Hills Mining Museum
323 West Main Street
P.O. Box 694
Lead, SD 57754
Phone: (605) 584-1605
E-mail: bhminmus@mato.com
www.mining-museum.blackhills.com

**Open:** All year. May–August 9:00 A.M.–5:00 P.M. daily; September–May 9:00 A.M.–4:30 P.M. Monday–Friday.

**Info:** The Black Hills Mining Museum is dedicated to the preservation of the rich mining heritage of the Black Hills of South Dakota. The museum offers tours of a simulated underground mine, exhibits, displays, photos, and artifacts to explain the mining process. Gold panning is offered at an additional cost. The underground mine is a re-creation of an underground level of the Homestake Mine, complete with over 20 full-size displays. During the tour you will explore a stope; witness a simulated blast; and see an underground cage station, powder and cap magazines, mine locomotives and ore cars, and much more. The museum also offers video presentations on changes in mining techniques over the past century.

**Admission:** Adults $5.50, seniors (60+) $5.00, children (7–college) $4.50; family rate $16.00. Children under 6 free. Optional museum activity of gold panning, $4.50-$5.00/person.

**Directions:** Lead is located on U.S. 85, south of I-90.

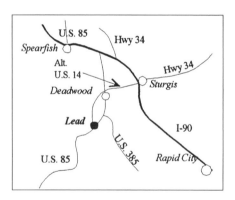

Phone: (605) 584-3110; (888) 701-0164
E-mail: hvc@mato.com
www.homestaketour.com

**Open:** September–May, 8:00 A.M.–5:00 P.M., Monday–Friday. June–August, 8:00 A.M.–5:00 P.M., Monday–Friday, 10:00 A.M.–5:00 P.M. Saturday and Sunday. Tours available 8:30 A.M.–4:30 P.M., every half hour, May–September only.

**Info:** Homestake is more than a museum; it is the world's oldest continuously operated gold mine. A tour of the Homestake offers the opportunity to witness the changes in American gold mining from the early days of panning to current high-tech mining. Through displays and mining artifacts, you will learn about mining and ore processing as well as about the mine, which extends more than 8,000 feet below the town of Lead. On completion of the tour you will receive a sample of ore that was drilled from the mine.

**Admission:** Adults $6.00, seniors $5.25, students (6–18) $5.00, children 5 and under free. Family rate $20.00.

**Other services available:** Gift shop.

**Directions:** The visitor center is located at the end of Main Street on the left.

## LEAD

## Museum/Surface Gold Mine Tour  🏛

Homestake Visitor Center
160 West Main Street
Lead, SD 57754-0887

## MURDO

## Museum  🏛

National Rockhound and Lapidary Hall of Fame
Pioneer Auto Show
I-90 and U.S. 83

Murdo, SD 57559-9215
Phone: (605) 669-2691
Fax: (605) 669-3217
www.rockhoundhalloffame.org

**Open:** Year round; hours may vary. Call ahead.

**Info:** The National Rockhound Hall of Fame was dedicated on June 15, 1987. The hall recognizes rockhounds and lapidaries, both living and dead, who have had great influence on the hobby. The Zeitner Gem, Mineral, and Fossil Collection, an extensive collection, is on display at the hall. There is a good variety of minerals, including one 8-foot display of minerals collected in South Dakota. The lapidary cases have a mixture of interesting materials, such as agates from most of the U.S. states, Mexico, and Australia. There are also examples of different lapidary techniques, including pictures, cabochons, sculptures, a fluorescent case, and a case of spheres.

**Admission:** Adults $8.50, children (6–13) $4.25, children (under 6) free.

**Other services available:** The hall is part of the Pioneer Auto and Antique Town (25 buildings).

**Directions:** Located in the Pioneer Auto Show off of Exit 192 on I-90, in Murdo.

## RAPID CITY

## Museum

Journey Museum
222 New York Street
Rapid City, SD 57701

Phone: (605) 394-6923
www.journeymuseum.org

**Open:** Memorial Day–Labor Day, daily, 9:00 A.M.–5:00 P.M. Winter, Monday–Saturday, 10:00 A.M.–5:00 P.M., Sundays 1:00 P.M.–5:00 P.M. Closed major holidays.

**Info:** Discover the earth's deepest secrets in the Museum of Geology. Displays show how the Black Hills were formed.

**Rates:** Adults $7.00, seniors $6.00, students 11–17 $5.00, children under 11 free. Call for group rates.

**Directions:** Contact the museum for directions.

## RAPID CITY

## Museum

South Dakota School of Mines and Technology
Museum of Geology
501 East St. Joseph Street
Rapid City, SD 57701
Phone: (605) 394-2467;
(800) 554-8162, ext. 2467
www.sdsmt.edu/services/museum

**Open:** All year; closed holidays. Memorial Day–Labor Day, Monday–Saturday 8:00 A.M.–6:00 P.M. Sunday 12:00–6:00 P.M. Rest of the year, Monday–Friday 8:00 A.M.–5:00 P.M., Saturday 9:00 A.M.–4:00 P.M., Sunday 1:00–4:00 P.M.

**Info:** Specializes in local specimens including minerals from the Black Hills, such as Fairborn agates, stibnite, and gypsum crystals.

**Admission:** Free.

**Directions:** Take West Boulevard south from I-90 to Main Street. Take Main Street east to the School of Mines.

---

## SECTION 3: Special Events and Tourist Information

---

## TOURIST INFORMATION

### State Tourist Agency

South Dakota Department of Tourism and State Development
711 East Wells Avenue
Pierre, SD 57501-3369
Phone: (800) SDAKOTA (732-5682);
(800) 952-3625
www.travelsd.com

# WASHINGTON

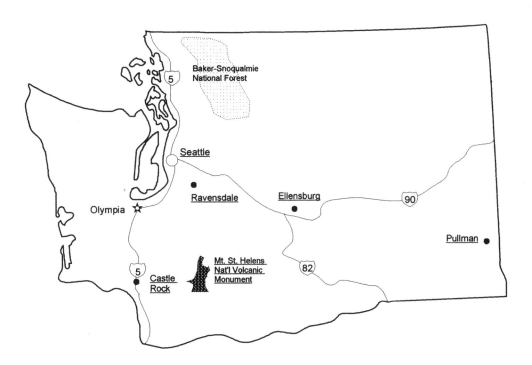

**State Gemstone:** Petrified Wood (1975)

## RAVENSDALE / *Native*

### Find pyrite, quartz, and other gems and minerals

*The following gems or minerals may be found:*

- Pyrite, quartz crystals, garnets, pink topaz, fluorite, barite, fluorescent minerals, amber, plant fossils, and fossil clams

Bob Jackson's Geology Adventures
P.O. Box 809
Ravensdale, WA 98051
Phone/Fax: (425) 413-1122

E-mail: bob@geologyadventures.com
(*Note:* often in the field for weeks at a time so it may take a while to get a return e-mail.)
www.geologyadventures.com

**Open:** Between July and September; must be scheduled in advance.
**Info:** A variety of tours are available, including ones geared toward kids. Offers tours in Pacific Northwest, British Columbia, and Australia.
**Rates:** Call for rates.
**Directions:** Call for directions.

## CASTLE ROCK

### Volcanic Monument 🏛

Mount St. Helens National
Volcanic Monument Visitor's Center
Monument Headquarters
42218 NE Yale Bridge Road
Amboy, WA 98601
Phone: (360) 449-7800
Fax: (360) 449-7801
www.fs.fed.us/gpnf/mshnvm

**Open:** All year, 8:00 A.M.–5:00 P.M. Monday–Friday.
**Info:** Other locations within the national monument are not open all year. They are open on weekends as well as weekdays, and may have different hours than the headquarters.

Many of the gems and minerals discussed in this book were formed as a result of volcanic activity. At Mount St. Helens in Washington, visitors can witness the power of the volcano. On May 18, 1980, Mount St. Helens erupted explosively, after 120 years of quiet. When the eruption was over, the top 1,300 feet of the mountain was gone. Several visitor centers have been constructed, providing views and interpretations of the eruption, along with displays, some of which focus on geology.

**Admission:** Adults $3.00, children 15

Mineral prospecting, such as gold panning, is allowed in Baker-Snoqualmie National Forest with a permit from the Washington Department of Fish and Wildlife. Some recreational mining activities are permitted by carrying a pamphlet (The Gold and Fish Pamphlet as revised in 1998) with you and following its guidance. You can obtain a copy of the Gold and Fish Pamphlet from:

Washington Department of Fish and Wildlife
Habitat and Lands Management Program
600 Capitol Way N.
Olympia, WA 98501-1091
Phone: (360) 902-2534

and under free (for one-day pass).

**Directions:** The National Volcanic Monument, which is located near the Washington-Oregon border, can be reached from I-5. State Highways 503, 504, and 505, and U.S. 12, provide access to different areas.

## ELLENSBURG

## Museum

Kittitas County Historical Museum and Society
114 East Third
Ellensburg, WA 98926-0265
Phone: (509) 925-3778
www.kchm.org

**Open:** All year, Monday–Saturday, 10:00 A.M.–4:00 P.M.

**Info:** The museum houses the vast collection of polished rock and petrified wood belonging to the Rollinger Brothers, who donated the collection to the citizens of Kittitas County.

**Admission:** Free; donations accepted.

**Directions:** Ellensburg is located at the intersection of I-90 and I-82. Call for directions to the museum.

## PULLMAN

## Museum

Washington State University
Department of Geology
Physical Science Building
Pullman, WA 99164-2812
Phone: (509) 335-3009

**Open:** When school is in session. Academic year hours: Monday–Friday 8:00 A.M.–5:00 P.M. Summer hours: Monday–Friday 7:30 A.M.–4:00 P.M.

Group tours available on weekends by prior reservations.

**Info:** The Lyle and Lela Jacklin collection of silicified wood and minerals is on display in the Harold E. Culver Memorial Room (Room 124) in the Physical

Science Building. The collection contains over 1,700 specimens collected from key sites in the western United States.

**Admission:** Free.

**Directions:** Call for directions to the university.

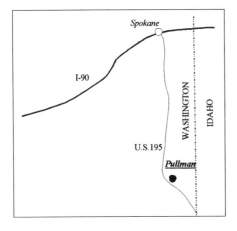

## SEATTLE

## Museum 🏛

Burke Museum of Natural History
University of Washington
Box 353010
Seattle, WA 98195-3010

Phone: (206) 543-5590
E-mail: receipt@uwashington.edu
www.burkemuseum.org

**Open:** Daily, 10:00 A.M.–5:00 P.M.; first Thursday of each month, 10: 00 A.M.–8:00 P.M.

**Info:** Exhibits present the historical geology of Washington, as well as a walk-through volcano, to give you the "inside" story. Also has rocks and minerals on display.

**Admission:** Adults $8.00, seniors $6.50, students $5.00, children under 6 free.

**Directions:** From I-5, take NE 45th Street exit east. Parking is available just south of the university campus.

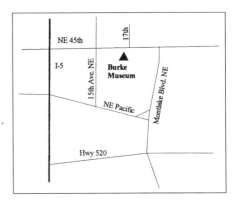

# SECTION 3: Special Events and Tourist Information

## TOURIST INFORMATION

## State Tourist Agency 🦫

Washington State Tourism
Phone: (800) 544-1800
www.experiencewashington.com

# WYOMING

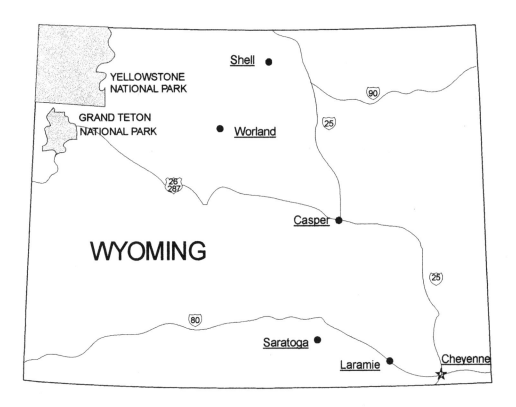

**State Gemstone:** Nephrite Jade (1967)

# SECTION 1: Fee Dig Sites and Guide Services

**SHELL /** *Native · Easy to Difficult*

## Dig for Moss Agate *T*

*The following gems or minerals may be found:*

▪ Dendritic agate

Trapper Galloway Ranch
Floyd "Kit" Smith
P.O. Box 95
Shell, WY 82441
Phone: (307) 765-2971
E-mail: kit@trappergallowayranch.com
www.trappergallowayranch.com

**Open:** Mine open after July 1, 7 days/ week.

**Info:** The mine is up in the Bighorns at approximately 8,400 feet elevation. You can dig for agate at the mine, or a pile of mined material is kept at the ranch. This

material can be picked through, and you can keep all that you find.

**Fee for the mine:** $150.00/day; keep all the material you want. Any material kept from the pile at the ranch will be charged $1.00/pound.

**Directions:** The ranch is located 1½ miles west of Shell.

# SECTION 2: Museums and Mine Tours

## CASPER

### Museum

Tate Geological Museum
Casper College
125 College Drive
Casper, WY 82601
Phone: (307) 268-2447
E-mail: dbrown@caspercollege.edu
www.caspercollege.edu/tate/webpage.asp

**Open:** All year, 9:00 A.M.–5:00 P.M. Monday–Friday; 10:00 A.M.–4:00 P.M. Saturday. Closed Sundays and major holidays.

**Info:** The museum has exhibits of rocks and minerals, including a display of Wyoming jade and a display of fluorescent minerals.

**Admission:** Free.

**Other services available:** Gift shop.

**Directions:** Take Wolcott Avenue south from Yellowstone Highway (U.S. 20) to

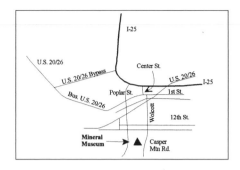

the Casper College Campus. Follow Wolcott to Casper Mountain Road (Highway 261) along campus; take the third right after College Drive onto Josendal Drive, then first right to the Tate Museum.

## CHEYENNE

## Museum

Wyoming State Museum
Barrett Building
2301 Central Avenue
Cheyenne, WY 82002
Phone: (307) 777-7022
Fax: (307) 777-5375
E-mail: wsm@state.wy.us
www.wyomuseumstate.wy.us

**Open:** May–October: Tuesday–Saturday 9:00 A.M.–4:30 P.M. November–April: Tuesday–Friday 9:00 A.M.–4:30 P.M., Saturday 10:00 A.M.–2:00 P.M. Closed state and federal holidays.
**Info:** The Swamped With Coal gallery addresses trona, coal, the evolution of mining lamps, jade (nephrite), gold, diamonds, oil, natural gas, uranium, and bentonite. Special features include a swamp to coal

mine model and an ore cart filled with examples of products visitors may have in their homes that are made with Wyoming raw materials; e.g., kitty litter is made from bentonite. The spin cubes are a hands-on activity which allows visitors to line up a mineral, the location it is found in the state, and what it is used to make.
**Admission:** Free.
**Other services available:** Museum store.
**Directions:** The museum is located on Central Avenue, one block south and east of the Wyoming State Capitol building.

## LARAMIE

## Museum

Geological Museum
University of Wyoming
Dept. 3006
1000 E. University Avenue
Laramie, WY 82071
Phone: (307) 766-2646
www.uwyo.edu/geomuseum

**Open:** All year, 8:00 A.M.–5:00 P.M., Monday–Friday. Weekends, 10:00 A.M.–3:00 P.M. Closed University holidays.
**Info:** The museum has exhibits of rocks

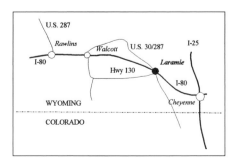

and minerals, including a display of fluorescent minerals from Wyoming and from around the world.

**Admission:** Free.

**Directions:** In the northwest corner of the university campus, next to the S.H. Knight Geology Building.

## SARATOGA

## Museum

Saratoga Museum
P.O. Box 1131
Saratoga, WY 82331
Phone: (307) 326-5511
E-mail: saratogamuseum@carbon
power.net
www.saratoga-museum.org

**Open:** Seasonal hours, Tuesday–Saturday 1:00 P.M.–4:00 P.M.

**Info:** Minerals from around the world and educational displays of local geology.

**Admission:** Call for current rates.

**Directions:** Take the Route 130 exit off I-80 at Walcott, and drive south (or east) on 130 to Saratoga, or take Route 130 west (or north) from Laramie. Located at 104 Constitution Avenue.

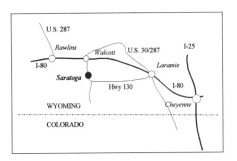

## WORLAND

## Museum

Washakie Museum
1115 Obie Sue
Worland, WY 82401
Phone: (307) 347-4784 or (307) 347-4102
Fax: (307) 347-4865
E-mail: washakiemuseum@rtconnect.net
www.washakiemuseum.com/

**Open:** Summer hours are from 9:00 A.M.–7:00 P.M., Tuesday–Friday; winter hours are from 10:00 A.M.–4:00 P.M., Tuesday–Saturday.

**Info:** Geology of the Big Horn Basin.

**Admission:** Free.

**Directions:** Call for directions.

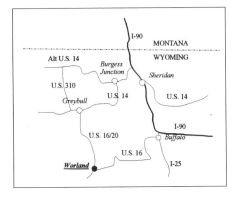

# SECTION 3: Special Events and Tourist Information

## ANNUAL EVENT

### Symposium

A Symposium on Wyoming geology and a field trip is held each June. For more information:

Tate Geological Museum
Casper College
125 College Drive
Casper, WY 82601
Phone: (307) 268-2447

## TOURIST INFORMATION

### State Tourist Agency

Wyoming Travel and Tourism
I-25 at College Drive
Cheyenne, WY 82002
Phone: (800) 225-5996; (307) 777-7777
www.state.wy.us

# Index by State

## ALABAMA

Fee Dig Mines and Guide Services
    None

Museums and Mine Tours

**Anniston**    Anniston Museum of Natural History—gemstones, meteorite, artificial indoor cave

**Dora**    Alabama Mining Museum—Focus on coal mining

**Tuscaloosa**    Alabama Museum of Natural History—minerals, meteorite

## ALASKA

Fee Dig Mines and Guide Services

**Anchorage**    Alaska DNR—Pan for gold
    Chugach National Forest—Pan for gold

**Fairbanks**    El Dorado Gold Mine—gold panning
    Faith Creek Camp—Pan, sluice, dredge for gold
    Gold Dredge No. 8—gold panning
    Chena Hot Springs Resort—gold panning

**Girdwood**    Crow Creek Mine—Pan for gold

**McGrath**    Moore Creek Mining, LLC—Prospect or dredge for gold

**Nome**    Nome Beaches—Pan for gold

**Talkeetna**    Clark/Wiltz Mining—Prospect for gold

**Wrangell**    St. Elias National Park and Preserve—Pan for gold, hunt for minerals

Museums and Mine Tours

**Chicken**    The Chicken Gold Camp & Outpost—Gold dredge tour

**Fairbanks**    El Dorado Gold Mine—working gold mine tour
    Gold Dredge No. 8—gold dredge tour
    University of Alaska Museum—minerals and gems from Alaska, Arctic Canada, and the Pacific Rim; includes gold and meteorites

| Juneau | Juneau–Douglas City Museum—History of gold mining |
| | Alaska Gastineau Mill and Gold Mine—Mine tour |
| **Nome** | The Carrie N. McLain Memorial Museum—History of gold mining |
| **Wasilla** | Independence Mine State Historical Park—Mine tour |

## ARIZONA

### Fee Dig Mines and Guide Services

| | |
| --- | --- |
| **Apache Jct.** | Apache Trails Tours—Gold panning |
| **Glendale** | William Gardner—Guide service |
| **Goldfield** | Goldfield Ghost Town, Scenic Railroad, and Mine Tours—Gold panning |
| **Prescott** | Lynx Creek Mineral Withdrawal Area, Prescott National Forest—Pan for gold |
| **Safford** | Black Hills Rockhound Area—Dig for fire agates |
| | Round Hill Rockhound Area—Search for fire agates, chalcedony, small geodes. |
| **Tempe** | Fat Jack Mine—Collect amethyst, quartz, garnet, tourmaline, limonite |
| **Wickenburg** | Robson's Mining World—Pan for gold |

### Museums and Mine Tours

| | |
| --- | --- |
| **Apache Jct.** | Superstition Mountain Museum—Geology, minerals, and mining |
| **Bisbee** | Queen Mine Tour—Tour a copper mine |
| **Flagstaff** | Meteor Crater Enterprises, Inc.—View a meteor crater, museum of astrogeology |
| | Museum of Northern Arizona—History of Colorado Plateau, geologic models, mineral specimens |
| **Goldfield** | Goldfield Ghost Town, Scenic Railroad, and Mine Tours—Gold mine tour, museum, ghost town |
| **Morenci** | Phelps Dodge Morenci Copper Mine—Tour an open-pit mine |
| **Phoenix** | Arizona Mining and Mineral Museum—3,000 minerals on exhibit, minerals from AZ copper mines, piece of meteor crater meteorite, rocks from original moon landing, spheres, fluorescent mineral display |
| **Sahuarita** | ASARCO Mineral Discovery Center—Geology, mining, minerals, and tour of open-pit mine |
| **Sun City** | The Mineral Museum—3,000 rocks and minerals from the U.S. and the world, with emphasis on minerals from AZ; Over 150 fluorescent rocks and minerals, most from Franklin and Sterling Hill, NJ |
| **Tempe** | Robert S. Dietz Museum of Geology—Mineral displays, seismograph |

| | |
|---|---|
| **Tucson** | Arizona-Sonora Desert Museum—Mineral collection from Sonoran desert region |
| | Mineral Museum, University of Arizona—2,100 of 15,000 minerals on display; AZ minerals, meteorites, fluorescents, borate minerals |
| **Wickenburg** | Robson's Mining World—Tour old gold mining village |
| | Vulture Gold Mine—Mine tour |

## Annual Events

| | |
|---|---|
| **Quartzsite** | Gem & Mineral Shows—Mid-January–mid-February |
| **Scottsdale** | Minerals of Arizona—Symposium 1 day in March |
| **Tucson** | Gem & Mineral Shows—First 2 weeks in February |

## ARKANSAS

### Fee Dig Mines and Guide Services

| | |
|---|---|
| **Hot Springs** | Coleman's Crystal Mines—Dig for quartz crystals |
| **Jessieville** | Jim Coleman Crystal Mines—Dig for quartz crystals |
| | Ouachita National Forest, Crystal Mt. Quartz Collecting Site—Collect quartz crystals |
| **Mt. Ida** | Fiddler's Ridge Rock Shop and Crystal Mines—Dig for quartz crystals |
| | Leatherhead Quartz Mining—Dig for quartz crystals |
| | Ouachita National Forest, Crystal Vista Quartz Collecting Site—Collect quartz crystals |
| | Sonny Stanley's Crystal Mine—Dig for quartz crystals |
| | Starfire Mine—Dig for quartz crystals |
| | Sweet Surrender Crystal Mine—Dig for quartz crystals |
| | Wegner's Crystal Mine—Dig for quartz crystals |
| **Murfreesboro** | Crater of Diamonds State Park—Dig and screen for diamonds, amethyst, agates, barite, calcite, jasper, quartz, other gems |
| **Pencil Bluff** | Arrowhead Crystal Mine—Dig for quartz crystals |

### Museums and Mine Tours

| | |
|---|---|
| **Fayetteville** | The University Museum—Quartz and other AR minerals |
| **Little Rock** | Geology Learning Center—AR gems, minerals, fossil fuels |
| **State University** | A.S.U. Museum—Minerals, many from AR |

### Annual Events

| | |
|---|---|
| **Mt. Ida** | Quartz Crystal Festival and World Championship Dig—Second weekend in October |

## CALIFORNIA

### Fee Dig Mines and Guide Services

**Angels Camp**   Jensen's Pick & Shovel Ranch—Guided prospecting for gold

**Coloma**   Marshall Gold Digging State Historic Park—Gold panning

**Columbia**   Hidden Treasures Gold Mine Tours—Gold panning

**Jackson**   Kennedy Gold Mine—Gold panning

**Jamestown**   Gold Prospecting Adventures, LLC—Gold panning

**Lakeport**   Lake County Visitors Information Center—Search for Lake County "diamonds" or "moon tears"

**Mariposa**   Little Valley Inn—Gold panning

**Mesa Grande**   Himalayan Tourmaline Mine—Look for California tourmaline

**Nevada City**   Malakoff Diggins State Historical Park—Gold panning

**Pala**   Ocean View Gem Mine—Hunt for tourmaline (pink, green, bicolor, and black); smoky crystals; garnets; book mica; smokey crystals; cleavelandite; kunzite; morganite, gossanite; purple lepidolite; muscovite mica; aquamarine

**Pine Grove**   Roaring Camp Mining Co.—Pan for gold, rockhounding

**Placerville**   Gold Bug Mine and Hangtown's Gold Bug Park—Gold panning

### Museums and Mine Tours

**Allegany**   Underground Gold Miners Tours and Museum—Tour an active gold mine

**Angels Camp**   Angels Camp Museum—Rocks and minerals; gold stamping mill, mining equipment

**Avalon**   Catalina Island Museum Society Inc.—Exhibits on mining on Catalina Island

**Boron**   Borax Global Visitors Center—Story of borax

Boron Twenty Mule Team Museum—History of area borate mining

**Coloma**   Marshall Gold Discovery State Historic Park—Gold mining exhibit/museum

**Columbia**   Hidden Treasure Gold Mine—Tour of active gold mine

**Death Valley**   Furnace Creek Borax Museum—Rocks and minerals, featuring borax minerals

**El Cajon**   Heritage of the Americas Museum—Rocks, minerals, and meteorites

**Fallbrook**   Fallbrook Gem & Mineral Museum—Gems and minerals

**Grass Valley**   Empire Mine State Historic Park—Hardrock gold mine

**Independence**   Eastern California Museum—Exhibit depicts local mining

| | |
|---|---|
| **Jackson** | Amador County Museum—Collection of mineral spheres from CA, UT, NV |
| | Kennedy Gold Mine Tours—Surface tour of gold mine |
| **Julian** | Eagle and High Peak Gold Mine Tours—Hardrock gold mine tour |
| | Julian Pioneer Museum—Rock and mineral display, gold mining tools and equipment displays |
| **Lucerne** | Lake County Museum—Minerals and gems from Lake County, CA |
| **Los Angeles** | Natural History Museum of Los Angeles County—52,000 specimens; minerals of CA; native gold, gems, and minerals |
| **Mariposa** | California State Mining and Mineral Museum—Gold from CA, gems and minerals from around the world |
| **Needles** | Needles Regional Museum—Needles blue agate, Colorado River pebble terrace stones |
| **Nevada City** | Malakoff Diggins State Historic Park—History of hydraulic gold mining |
| **Pacific Grove** | Pacific Grove Museum of Natural History—Monterey County rocks, fluorescent minerals |
| **Paso Robles** | El Paso des Robles Area Pioneer Museum—Display of local minerals |
| **Placerville** | Gold Bug Mine and Hangtown's Gold Bug Park—Tour hardrock gold mine |
| **Quincy** | Plumas County Museum—Exhibits on silver and copper mining in Plumas County |
| **Rancho Palo Verdes** | Point Vicente Interpretive Center—Exhibits on area geology |
| **Redlands** | San Bernardino County Museum—45,000 rocks, minerals, and gems |
| **Ridgecrest** | Maturango Museum—Small but well-rounded regional gem and mineral collection |
| **Riverside** | Jurupa Mountains Cultural Center—Crestmore minerals display, minerals from around the world on display and for sale, family education programs |
| | Riverside Municipal Museum—Rocks, minerals, gems, and regional geology |
| | World Museum of Natural History—Fluorescent minerals, meteorites, tektites, over 1,300 mineral spheres |
| **San Diego** | San Diego Natural History Museum—26,000 mineral specimens, includes minerals found in San Diego County mines |
| **Santa Barbara** | Department of Geological Sciences, U.C.S.B.—Gem and mineral collection, minerals and their tectonic settings |
| **Shoshone** | Shoshone Museum—Rock collection reflecting the geology of the area |
| **Sierra City** | Kentucky Mine and Museum—Exhibits of local gold and mercury mining |

| | |
|---|---|
| **Sonora** | Tuolomne County Museum—Gold from local mines |
| **Yermo** | Calico Ghost Town—Explore a silver mine |
| **Yreka** | Siskiyou County Courthouse—Gold exhibit |
| **Yucca Valley** | Hi-Desert Nature Museum—Rock and mineral collection, includes fluorescent minerals |

### Annual Events

| | |
|---|---|
| **Boron** | Rock Bonanza—Weekend before Easter |
| **Coloma** | Marshall Gold Discovery State Historic Park: Gold Rush Days—End of September–beginning of October |

## COLORADO

### Fee Dig Mines and Guide Services

| | |
|---|---|
| **Idaho Springs** | Argo Gold Mill—Pan for gold and gemstones |
| | Phoenix Mine—Pan for gold |

### Museums and Mine Tours

| | |
|---|---|
| **Colorado Springs** | Western Museum of Mining and Industry—Displays of mining and gold panning |
| **Cripple Creek** | Cripple Creek District Museum—Mineral displays |
| | Molly Kathleen Gold Mine—Gold mine tour |
| **Denver** | Denver Museum of Natural History—2,000 specimens, includes gold, topaz, aquamarine, amazonite, and other Colorado minerals |
| **Georgetown** | Lebanon Silver Mine—Tour a silver mine |
| **Golden** | Geology Museum, Colorado School of Mines—50,000 specimens, minerals from Colorado and from around the world, gemstones and precious metals, cave exhibit |
| **Idaho Springs** | Argo Gold Mill—Historic gold mill, mining museum, Double Eagle Gold Mine |
| | Edgar Experimental Mine—Tour an experimental mine (silver, gold, lead, copper) |
| | Phoenix Mine—See a working underground hardrock mine (gold, silver) |
| **Leadville** | Matchless Mine—Tour a gold mine |
| | National Mining Hall of Fame and Museum—Story of the American mining industry from coal to gold |
| **Ouray** | Ouray County Historical Society—Mineral and mining displays |
| **Salida** | Lost Mine Tour—Mangenese mine |
| **Silverton** | Mayflower Gold Mill—Tour a gold mill |
| | Old Hundred Gold Mine Tour, Inc.—Gold mine tour |

San Juan County Historical Museum—Minerals and gems from the Silverton area

**Victor**       Mine View—View of Colorado's largest open-pit gold mine

## CONNECTICUT

### Fee Dig Mines and Guide Services

**Roxbury**       Green's Farm Garnet Mine—Search for garnets

### Museums and Mine Tours

**East Granby**   Old New-Gate Prison and Copper Mine—Tour an old copper mine
**Greenwich**     Bruce Museum of Arts and Science—Minerals and rocks
**New Haven**     Peabody Museum of Natural History—Minerals of New England and the world

## DELAWARE

### Fee Dig Mines and Guide Services

None

### Museums and Mine Tours

**Newark**        Delaware Academy of Science, Iron Hill Museum—DE minerals, fluorescent minerals

University of Delaware, Mineralogical Museum—5,000 specimens (1,000 on display), crystals, gems, minerals

## DISTRICT OF COLUMBIA

### Fee Dig Mines and Guide Services

None

### Museums and Mine Tours

Smithsonian Institution, National Museum of Natural History—Gems and minerals

## FLORIDA

### Fee Dig Mines and Guide Services

**Ft. Drum**      Ft. Drum Crystal Mine (Ruck's Pit)—Collect calcite encrusted fossil shells

## Museums and Mine Tours

| | |
|---|---|
| **Deland** | Gillespie Museum, Stetson University—Minerals, gemstones, faceting, replica mine, and cave |
| **Mulberry** | Mulberry Phosphate Museum—Exhibits on the phosphate industry |
| **Tampa** | Ed and Bernadette Marcin Museum, University of Florida—Minerals and gemstones mainly from FL and the western U.S. |

## GEORGIA

### Fee Dig Mines and Guide Services

| | |
|---|---|
| **Cleveland** | Gold'n Gem Grubbin—Dig and pan for gold, sapphires, rubies, emeralds, amethyst, topaz |
| **Dahlonega** | Consolidated Gold Mine—Gold panning |
| | Crisson Gold Mine—Pan gold sands or enriched gemstone ore |
| **Gainesville** | Chattahooche-Oconee National Forest—Gold panning |
| **Helen** | Gold Mine of Helen, GA—Pan gold sand or enriched gemstone ore |
| **Jackson's Crossroads** | Dixie Euhedrals—Hunt for amethyst |
| **LaGrange** | Hogg Mine—Collect star rose quartz, aquamarine, beryl (rare), black tourmaline |
| **Lincolnton** | Graves Mountain—Search for audite, lazulite, pyrophyllite, kyanite, hematite, pyrite, ilmenite, muscovite, fuchsite, barite, sulfur, blue quartz, quartz crystals, microcrystals such as woodhouseite, variscite, strengite, phosphosiderite, cacoxenite, crandallite |

### Museums and Mine Tours

| | |
|---|---|
| **Atlanta** | Fernbank Museum of Natural History—Joachim gem collection containing 400 cut and polished gemstones |
| | Fernbank Science Center—Gems, carved opals, meteorites |
| **Cartersville** | Weinman Mineral Museum—2,000 specimens, gems and minerals from the state; simulated cave |
| **Dahlonega** | Consolidated Gold Mine—Mine tour |
| | Dahlonega Gold Museum—Tells the story of the GA Gold Rush |
| **Elberton** | Elberton Granite Museum—Granite quarry and products |
| **Helen** | Gold Mine of Helen, GA—Mine tour |
| **Macon** | Museum of Arts and Science—Display of gems and minerals |
| **Statesboro** | Georgia Southern Museum—Collection of rocks and minerals from Georgia's highlands, Piedmont, and coastal regions |
| **Tallapoosa** | West Georgia Museum of Tallapoosa—Small collection of local minerals |

Annual Events

**Jasper**          Pickens County Marble Festival—First weekend in October

## HAWAII

### Fee Dig Mines and Guide Services
None

### Museums and Mine Tours
**Hawaii Nat'l**    Thomas A. Jaggar Museum—Museum on vulcanology and seismol-
**Park**            ogy; tour of volcano
**Hilo**            Lyman House Memorial Museum—Rocks, minerals, gems

## IDAHO

### Fee Dig Mines and Guide Services
**Moscow**          3-D's Panhandle Gems and Garnet Queen Mine—Guide service, star
                    garnet digging; trips including gold panning.
**Spencer**         Spencer Opal Mine—Pick through a stockpile for fire opal; pre-
                    arranged digging at mine is a possibility
**St. Maries**      Emerald Creek Garnet Area—Dig for star garnets

### Museums and Mine Tours
**Boise**           Museum of Mining and Geology—Exhibits on mining and geology
**Caldwell**        The Glen L. and Ruth M. Evans Gem and Mineral Collection—
                    Agate, jasper, other gemstones, 2,000 cabochons
                    Orma J. Smith Museum of Natural History—Extensive collection of
                    minerals
**Kellogg**         Crystal Gold Mine—Mine tour
                    Staff House Museum—Rocks, minerals, mining equipment
**Pocatella**       Idaho Museum of Natural History—Displays of specimens from
                    Idaho and the intermountain west
**Wallace**         Sierra Silver Mine Tour—Mine tour

## ILLINOIS

### Fee Dig Mines and Guide Services
None

### Museums and Mine Tours
**Chicago**         The Field Museum—92-year-old gem exhibit

| | |
|---|---|
| **Elmhurst** | Lizzadro Museum of Lapidary Art—1,300 pieces of cut and polished gems, fluorescent rocks, a birthstone display |
| **Rockford** | Burpee Museum of Natural History—Displays of rocks, minerals, and gems |
| **Rock Island** | Augustana Fryxell Geology Museum—Rock and mineral musuem |
| **Rosiclare** | The American Fluorite Museum—Story of Fluorospur Industry |
| **Shirley** | The Funk Gem and Mineral Museum—Gem and mineral collection |
| **Springfield** | Illinois State Museum—Gems and minerals, Illinois specimens, birthstones, fluorescents, copper |
| **West Frankfort** | The National Coal Museum, Mine 25—Tour a shaft coal mine |

## INDIANA

### Fee Dig Mines and Guide Services

| | |
|---|---|
| **Knightstown** | Yogi Bear Jellystone Park Camping Resort—Midwestern gold prospecting |

### Museums and Mine Tours

| | |
|---|---|
| **Bedford** | Land of Limestone Exhibition—History of Indiana Limestone industry |
| **Fort Wayne** | Indiana Purdue University at Fort Wayne—Hallway displays of minerals, meteorites, and rocks |
| **Indianapolis** | Indiana State Museum—Indiana and regional minerals |
| **Richmond** | Joseph Moore Museum of Natural History, Earlham College—Geology exhibit from local Ordovician limestone |

## IOWA

### Fee Dig Mines and Guide Services

None

### Museums and Mine Tours

| | |
|---|---|
| **Danville** | Geode State Park—Display of geodes |
| **Iowa City** | University of Iowa—Displays on state geology |
| **Sioux City** | Sioux City Public Museum—Mineralogy exhibit |
| **Waterloo** | Grout Museum—Display of rocks and minerals |
| **West Bend** | Grotto of the Redemption—Grotto made of precious stones and gems |
| **Winterset** | Madison County Historical Society—Rock and mineral collection |

## KANSAS

### Fee Dig Mines and Guide Services
None

### Museums and Mine Tours
**Ashland**    Pioneer Krier Museum—Mineral exhibit

**Emporium**    Johnston Geology Museum—Tri-state mining display, geological specimens from Kansas

**Galena**    Galena Mining and Historical Museum—Focus on local lead mining and smelting industry

**Greensburg**    Pallasite Meteorite at the Big Well Museum—Meteorite strike site and 1,000-pound meteorite

**McPherson**    McPherson Museum—Meteorites

## KENTUCKY

### Fee Dig Mines and Guide Services
**Marion**    Clement Mineral Museum—Fluorite collecting pit

### Museums and Mine Tours
**Benham**    Kentucky Coal Mine Museum—Displays on coal mining and formation of coal

**Covington**    Behringen-Crawford Museum—Display of gems and minerals

**Lynch**    Lynch Portal 31 Walking Tour—Walking tour of coal mining facilities

**Marion**    The Clement Mineral Museum—Display of gems and minerals

## LOUISIANA

### Fee Dig Mines and Guide Services
None

### Museums and Mine Tours
**New Orleans**    Louisiana Nature Center—Small collection of gems and minerals

**Shreveport**    Louisiana State Exhibit Museum—Displays on mining and salt domes

## MAINE

### Fee Dig Mines and Guide Services
**Auburn**       City of Auburn/Feldspar and Greenlaw Quarries—Hunt for apatite, tourmaline, and quartz

Mt. Apatite Farm/Turner Quarry—Hunt for tourmaline, garnet, graphic granite, clevelandite

**Bethel**       Songo Pond Mine—Collect tourmaline and other ME gems and minerals

**Poland**       Poland Mining Camp—Collect tourmaline and other ME gems and minerals

**West Paris**   Perham's of West Paris—Collect tourmaline and other ME gems and minerals

### Museums and Mine Tours
**Augusta**      Maine State Museum—Gems and minerals of ME
**Caribou**      Nylander Museum—Minerals of Maine
**West Paris**   Perham's of West Paris—ME gems and minerals; model of a feldspar quarry, model of a gem tourmaline pocket, fluorescents

### Annual Events
**Augusta**      Maine Mineral Symposium—3rd weekend in May

## MARYLAND

### Fee Dig Mines and Guide Services
None

### Museums and Mine Tours
**Great Falls**  Maryland Mine Trail—Gold mine trail

## MASSACHUSETTS

### Fee Dig Mines and Guide Services
None

### Museums and Mine Tours
**Amherst**      Pratt Museum of Natural History—10,000 specimens; minerals from New England and around the world, meteorites

**Cambridge**    Harvard University Museum of Cultural and Natural History—Gems, minerals, ores, meteorites

**Springfield**  Springfield Science Museum—Minerals from around the world

## MICHIGAN

### Fee Dig Mines and Guide Services
**Mohawk**       Delaware Copper Mine—Search for souvenir copper

### Museums and Mine Tours
**Ann Arbor**       Exhibit Museum of Natural History, University of Michigan— Exhibits of rocks and minerals

**Bloomfield Hills** Cranbrook Institute of Science—5,000 minerals and crystals from around the world, including hiddenite, gold

**Calumet**       Mining Museum at Coppertown, U.S.A.—Exhibits on copper mining

**Caspian**       Iron County Museum and Park—Iron mining complex

**Chelsea**       Gerald E. Eddy Geology Center—MI rocks, minerals, crystals, and mining

**Copper Harbor** Fort Wilkins State Park—History of copper mining in the area

**Greenland**       Old Adventure Copper Mine—Tour underground copper mine

**Hancock**       The Quincy Mining Company—Tour an underground copper mine

**Houghton**       The Seaman Mineral Museum—Crystal collection, minerals from the Lake Superior copper district

**Hubbell**       The Caledonia Copper Mine—Collect copper, silver, epidote, calcite, hematite

**Iron Mountain** Iron Mountain Iron Mine—Iron mine tour

**Lake Linden**       Houghton County Historical Museum—Copper mining and refining equipment displays

**Mohawk**       Delaware Copper Mine—Mine tour

**Mount Pleasant**       Museum of Cultural and Natural History, Central Michigan University—MI rocks and minerals

**Negaunee**       Michigan Iron Industry Museum—Story of MI iron industry

## MINNESOTA

### Fee Dig Mines and Guide Services
              None

### Museums and Mine Tours
**Calumet**       Hill Annex Mine State Park—Tour an open pit iron mine

**Chisholm**       Ironworld Discovery Center—Iron industry taconite mining tours

              Minnesota Museum of Mining—Indoor and outdoor exhibits

              Taconite Mine Tours—Tour of an open-pit iron ore mine

**Hibbing**       Mahoning Hull-Rust Mine—Observe an open-pit iron mine

| | |
|---|---|
| **Pipestone** | Pipestone National Monument—Tour a Native American pipestone quarry |
| **Soudan** | Soudan Underground Mine State Park—Tour an underground iron mine |
| **Virginia** | Mineview in the Sky—View an open-pit iron ore mine |
| | Iron Trails Conventions and Visitor's Bureau—Information on mine view sites |

## MISSISSIPPI

### Fee Dig Mines and Guide Services
None

### Museums and Mine Tours
| | |
|---|---|
| **Starkville** | Dunn-Seiler Museum—Mineral and rock collections |

## MISSOURI

### Fee Dig Mines and Guide Services
| | |
|---|---|
| **Alexandria** | Sheffler Rock Shop—Dig geodes lined with crystals |

### Museums and Mine Tours
| | |
|---|---|
| **Golden** | Golden Pioneer Museum—Large mineral exhibit |
| **Joplin** | Everett J. Richie Tri-State Mineral Museum—Story of area's lead and zinc mining |
| **Kansas City** | University of Missouri–Kansas City, Geosciences Museum—Local and regional specimens |
| **Park Hills** | Missouri Mines State Historic Site—1,100 minerals, ores, and rocks |
| **Point Lookout** | Ralph Foster Museum, College of the Ozarks—Gemstone spheres and fluorescent minerals |
| **Rolla** | Mineral Museum, U. of Missouri, Rolla—3,500 minerals, ores, and rocks from 92 countries and 47 states |

## MONTANA

### Fee Dig Mines and Guide Services
| | |
|---|---|
| **Alder** | Red Rock Mine—Screen for garnets |
| **Clinton** | L◊E Guest Ranch Outfitters—Sapphire mining pack trips |
| **Dillon** | Crystal Park Recreational Mineral Collecting Area—Dig for quartz and amethyst crystal |
| **Hamilton** | Sapphire Studio—Sapphire mining "parties" |

| | |
|---|---|
| **Helena** | Spokane Bar Sapphire Mine and Gold Fever Rock Shop—Dig and screen for sapphires and other gems and minerals |
| **Libby** | Libby Creek Recreational Gold Panning Area—Pan for gold |
| **Philipsburg** | Gem Mountain—Search for sapphires |
| | Sapphire Gallery—Wash bags of gravel to look for sapphires |

## Museums and Mine Tours

| | |
|---|---|
| **Butte** | Anselmo Mine Yard—Tour of mining facilities and history of area mining |
| | The Berkeley Pit—Observation point for closed open-pit copper mine |
| | Butte-Silver Bow Visitors and Transportation Center—Presents information on area geology and its mining, including local gold and silver mining |
| | Mineral Museum, Montana College of Mineral Science and Technology—Gold, fluorescents, and minerals from Butte and MT |
| | World Museum of Mining and 1899 Mining Camp—Tour of surface facilities of former silver and zinc mine |
| **Ekalaka** | Carter County Museum—Fluorescent mineral display |
| **Lewistown** | Central Montana Museum—Rocks, minerals, and yogo sapphires |

## NEBRASKA

### Fee Dig Mines and Guide Services
None

### Museums and Mine Tours

| | |
|---|---|
| **Chadron** | Eleanor Barbour Cook Museum of Geoscience—Displays of rocks and minerals |
| **Crawford** | Trailside Museum—Displays of western Nebraska geology |
| **Hastings** | Hastings Museum—Minerals, rocks, fluorescent minerals, and translucent slabs |
| **Lincoln** | University of Nebraska State Museum—Displays of rocks, minerals and fluorescent rocks |

## NEVADA

### Fee Dig Mines and Guide Services

| | |
|---|---|
| **Denio** | Bonanza Opal Miles, Inc.—Dig fire wood opal |
| | The Opal Queen Mining Company—Dig crystal, white, and black fire opal |

Rainbow Ridge Opal Mine—Tailings digging for wood opal

Royal Peacock Opal Mine, Inc.—Dig black and fire opal

**Ely**  Garnet Fields Rockhound Area—Hunt for garnets

**Reno**  High Desert Gems and Minerals—Gem mine tours

## Museums and Mine Tours

**Las Vegas**  Nevada State Museum and Historical Society—Natural history of Nevada

**Reno**  W.M. Keck Earth Science and Mineral Engineering Museum—Collection of minerals and ores

**Virginia City**  Chollar Mine—Underground mine tour (gold and silver mine)

## NEW HAMPSHIRE

### Fee Dig Mines and Guide Services

**Grafton**  Ruggles Mine—Collect up to 150 different minerals

**Laconia**  White Mountain National Forest—Collect amethyst, quartz, and mica

### Museums and Mine Tours

**Dover**  The Woodman Institute—1,300 specimens, including local rocks

## NEW JERSEY

### Fee Dig Mines and Guide Services

**Cape May**  Cape May Welcome Center—Hunt for Cape May "diamonds"

**Franklin**  Franklin Mineral Museum and Buckwheat Dump—Tailings diggings for fluorescent minerals and franklinite

**Ogdenburg**  Sterling Hill Mine and Museum—Collect minerals

### Museums and Mine Tours

**Franklin**  Franklin Mineral Museum—Minerals, rocks, local and worldwide fluorescents

**Monroe Township**  Displayworld's Stone Museum—Minerals, hands-on exhibits

**Morristown**  Morristown Museum—Specimens from five continents

**New Brunswick**  Rutgers Geology Museum—Specimens from the zinc deposit at Franklin and the zeolite deposits from Paterson, meteorites

**Ogdensburg**  Sterling Hill Mine and Museum—Tour old zinc mine

**Paterson**  The Paterson Museum—Specimens from local basalt flows and basalt flow in the Poona region of India, minerals from NJ and around the world

| **Rutherford** | Meadowland Museum—Fluorescent minerals, quartz, minerals from NJ |
| **Trenton** | New Jersey State Museum—Minerals and rocks, including fluorescents and magnetite ore |

Annual Events

| **Franklin** | New Jersey Earth Science Association Gem and Mineral Show and Outdoor Swap & Sell—Late April |

## NEW MEXICO

Fee Dig Mines and Guide Services

| **Bingham** | Blanchard Mines—Collect over 84 different kinds of minerals in a former lead mine |
| **Deming** | Rockhound State Park—Collect a variety of semiprecious stones |
| **Dixon** | Harding Mine—Harding pegmatite has yielded over 50 minerals |
| **Magdalena** | Bill's Gems & Minerals—Collect copper and iron minerals at mine dumps |

Museums and Mine Tours

| **Albuquerque** | Geology Museum, University of New Mexico—Displays of NM minerals and geology |
| | Institute of Meteoritics, University of New Mexico—Meteorites |
| | New Mexico Museum of Natural History and Science—3,000 specimens with a focus on NM and the southwestern U.S. |
| | The Turquoise Museum—Turquoise museum |
| **Portales** | Miles Mineral Museum—Dispays of minerals, gems, and meteorites |
| **Socorro** | New Mexico Bureau of Mines and Mineral Resources—10,000 specimens of minerals from NM, the U.S., and the world |

Annual Events

| **Socorro** | New Mexico Mineral Symposium |

## NEW YORK

Fee Dig Mines and Guide Services

| **Herkimer** | Herkimer Diamond Mine and KOA Kampground—Dig for Herkimer "Diamonds" |
| **Middleville** | Ace of Diamonds Mine and Campground—Prospect for Herkimer "Diamonds," calcite crystals, and dolomite crystals |
| **North River** | Barton Mines—Hunt for garnets |

**St. Johnsville**    Crystal Grove Diamond Mine and Campground—Dig for Herkimer "Diamonds"

### Museums and Mine Tours
**Albany**       New York State Museum—Minerals from New York
**Hicksville**   The Hicksville Gregory Museum—9,000 specimens form the major minerals groups; also NJ zeolites, Herkimer "diamonds," fluorescents
**New York**     American Museum of Natural History—Gems, meteorites; emphasis on exceptional specimens from the U.S.
**Pawling**      The Gunnison Natural History Museum—Minerals

## NORTH CAROLINA

### Fee Dig Mines and Guide Services
**Almond**       Nantahala Gorge Ruby Mine—Sluice for rubies, sapphires, amethyst, topaz, garnet, citrine, smoky quartz
**Boone**        Foggy Mountain Gem Mine—Screen for topaz, garnet, aquamarine, peridot, ruby, star sapphire, amethyst, citrine, smoky quartz, tourmaline, emerald
**Canton**       Old Pressley Sapphire Mine—Sluice for sapphires
**Cherokee**     Smoky Mountain Gold & Ruby Mine—Sluice for gold and gems
**Chimney Rock** Chimney Rock Gemstone Mine—Screen for aquamarine, emerald, ruby, peridot, garnet, quartz, agate, hematite, amethyst, sodalite
**Franklin**     Cowee Mountain Ruby Mine—Sluice for rubies, sapphires, garnets, tourmaline, smoky quartz, amethyst, citrine, moonstone, topaz

Gold City Gem Mine—Sluice for rubies, sapphires, garnets, emeralds, tourmaline, smoky quartz, amethyst, citrine, moonstone, topaz

Mason Mountain Rhodolite and Ruby Mine and Cowee Gift Shop—Sluice for rhodolite, rubies, sapphires, garnets, kyanite, crystal quartz, smoky quartz, moonstones

Masons Ruby and Sapphire Mine—Dig and sluice for sapphires (all colors), pink and red rubies

Moonstone Gem Mine—Sluice for rhodolite, rubies, sapphires, garnets, other precious stones

Rocky Face Gem Mine—Sluice for rubies, rhodolite garnets

Rose Creek Mine, Campground, Trout Pond, and Rock Shop—Sluice for rubies, sapphires, garnets, moonstones, amethysts, smoky quartz, citrine, rose quartz, topaz

Sheffield Mine—Sluice for rubies, sapphires, enriched material from around the world

| | |
|---|---|
| **Hiddenite** | Emerald Hollow Mine, Hiddenite Gems, Inc.—Rutile, sapphires, garnets, monazite, hiddenite, smoky quartz, tourmaline, clear quartz, aquamarine, sillimanite |
| **Highlands** | Jackson Hole Gem Mine—Sluice for rubies, sapphires, garnets, tourmaline, smoky quartz, amethyst, citrine, moonstone, topaz |
| **Little Switzerland** | Blue Ridge Gemstone Mine & Campground—Sapphire, emeralds, rubies, aquamarine, tourmaline, topaz, garnets, amethysts, lepidolite, citrine, moonstone, kyanite, and rose, clear, rutilated, and smoky quartz |
| | Emerald Village—Sapphire, emeralds, rubies, aquamarine, tourmaline, topaz, garnets, amethysts, lepidolite, citrine, beryl, moonstone, kyanite, and rose, clear, rutilated, and smoky quartz |
| **Marion** | The Lucky Strike—Gems and gold panning |
| | Carolina Emerald Mine and Vein Mountain Gold Camp—Mine for gold, emerald, aquamarine, moonstone, feldspar crystals, garnets, smoky, rose, blue and clear quartz, and tourmaline |
| **Marshall** | Little Pine Garnet Mine—Dig for garnets |
| **Micaville** | Rock Mine Tours and Gift Shop—Dig for emeralds, aquamarine, golden beryl, feldspar, pink feldspar, star garnets, biotite, olivine, moonstone, thulite, and black tourmaline |
| **New London** | Cotton Patch Gold Mine—Gold panning |
| | Mountain Creek Gold Mine—Gold panning |
| **Spruce Pine** | Gem Mountain Gemstone Mine—Sapphires, crabtree emeralds, rubies, Wiseman aquamarine |
| | Rio Doce Gem Mine—Sapphires, emeralds, rubies, aquamarine, tourmaline, topaz, garnets, amethysts, lepidolite, citrine, beryl, moonstone, kyanite, and rose, clear, rutilated, and smoky quartz |
| | Spruce Pine Gem and Gold Mine—Sapphires, emeralds, rubies, aquamarine, tourmaline, topaz, garnets, amethysts, lepidolite, citrine, beryl, moonstone, kyanite, and rose, clear, rutilated, and smoky quartz |
| **Stanfield** | Reed Gold Mine Historic Site—Gold panning |
| **Union Mills** | Thermal City Gold Mining Company—Gold panning |

## Museums and Mine Tours

| | |
|---|---|
| **Asheville** | Colburn Earth Science Museum—Collection of mineral specimens from NC and the world |
| **Aurora** | Aurora Fossil Museum—Geology of phosphate mine |
| **Franklin** | Franklin Gem and Mineral Museum—Specimens from NC and around the world |
| | Ruby City Gems and Minerals—Specimens from NC and around the world |

| | |
|---|---|
| **Gastonia** | Schiele Museum—North Carolina gems and minerals |
| **Greensboro** | Natural Science Center of Greensboro—Specimens from NC and around the world |
| **Hendersonville** | Mineral and Lapidary Museum of Hendersonville, Inc.—Minerals and lapidary arts |
| **Linville** | Grandfather Mountain Nature Museum—Specimens from NC |
| **Little Switzerland** | North Carolina Mining Museum and Mine Tour—Tour a closed feldspar mine |
| **Spruce Pine** | Museum of North Carolina Minerals—Specimens primarily from local mines |
| **Stanfield** | Reed Gold Mine Historic Site—Gold mine tour |

## Annual Events

| | |
|---|---|
| **Franklin** | Macon County Gemboree—3rd weekend in July |
| | "Leaf Looker" Gemboree—2nd weekend in October |
| **Spruce Pine** | Original NC Mineral and Gem Festival—4 days at the beginning of August |

## NORTH DAKOTA

### Fee Dig Mines and Guide Services

None

### Museums and Mine Tours

| | |
|---|---|
| **Dickinson** | Dakota Dinosaur Museum—Rocks and minerals, including borax from CA, turquoise from AZ, fluorescents, aurora crystals from AR |

## OHIO

### Fee Dig Mines and Guide Services

| | |
|---|---|
| **Hopewell** | Hidden Springs Ranch—Dig for flint (groups only) |
| | Nethers Flint—Dig for flint |

### Museums and Mine Tours

| | |
|---|---|
| **Cleveland** | The Cleveland Museum of Natural History—The Wade Gallery of Gems and Minerals has over 1,500 gems and minerals |
| **Columbus** | Orton Geological Museum—Rocks and minerals from OH and the world |
| **Dayton** | Boonshoft Museum of Discovery—Minerals and crystals |
| **Glenford** | Flint Ridge State Memorial—Ancient flint quarrying |

**Lima**          Allen County Museum—Rock and mineral exhibit

## OKLAHOMA

### Fee Dig Mines and Guide Services
**Jet**          Salt Plains National Wildlife Refuge—Digging for selenite crystals
**Kenton**       Black Mesa Bed & Breakfast—Rockhounding on a working cattle ranch
                 Howard Layton Ranch—Rockhounding on a working cattle ranch

### Museums and Mine Tours
**Coalgate**     Coal Country Mining and Historical Museum—Mining museum
**Enid**         The Mr. and Mrs. Dan Midgley Museum—Rock and mineral collection predominantly from OK and the TX shoreline
**Noble**        Timberlake Rose Rock Museum—Displays of barite roses
**Picher**       Picher Mining Museum—Lead and zinc mining
**Tulsa**        Elsing Museum—Gems and minerals

### Annual Events
**Cherokee**     The Crystal Festival and Selenite Crystal Dig—First Saturday in May
**Noble**        Annual Rose Rock Festival—First Saturday in May

## OREGON

### Fee Dig Mines and Guide Services
**Federal lands**  (Baker City, Jacksonville, Medford, Salem, Unity)—Pan for gold

**Klamath Falls**  Juniper Ridge Opal Mine—Hunt for fire opal
**Madras**       Richards Recreational Ranch—Dig for thundereggs, agate
**Mitchell**     Lucky Strike Geodes—Dig for thundereggs (picture jasper)
**Plush**        Dust Devil Mining Co.—Dig for sunstones
                 High Desert Gems & Minerals—Dig for sunstones
**Roseburg**     Cow Creek Recreational Area—Pan for gold
**Yachats**      Beachcombing—Collect agates and jaspers

### Museums and Mine Tours
**Central Point**  Crater Rock Museum—Minerals, thundereggs, fossils, geodes, cut and polished gemstones
**Corvallis**    Oregon State University Dept. of Geosciences—Mineral displays
**Hillsboro**    Rice Northwest Museum of Rocks and Minerals—Displays of minerals and crystals

| | |
|---|---|
| **Redmond** | Peterson's Rock Garden—Unusual rock specimens, fluorescent display |
| **Sumpter** | Sumpter Valley Dredge State Historical Heritage Area—View a gold dredge, tour historic gold mine towns |

Annual Events

| | |
|---|---|
| **Cottage Grove** | Bohemia Mining Days—Four days in July, gold panning and exposition |
| **Prineville** | Rockhounds Pow-Wow—Mid-June |

## PENNSYLVANIA

Fee Dig Mines and Guide Services

| | |
|---|---|
| **Williamsport** | Crystal Point Diamond Mine—Dig for quartz crystals |

Museums and Mine Tours

| | |
|---|---|
| **Ashland** | Museum of Anthracite Mining—Story of anthracite coal |
| | Pioneer Tunnel Coal Mine—Tour an anthracite coal mine |
| **Bryn Mawr** | Museum, Department of Geology, Bryn Mawr College—Rotating display of 1,500 minerals from collection of 23,500 specimens |
| **Carlisle** | Rennie Geology Museum, Dickinson College—Gem and mineral display |
| **Harrisburg** | State Museum of Pennsylvania—Geology of everyday products |
| **Lancaster** | North Museum of Natural History and Science—Worldwide specimens with a focus on Lancaster County |
| **Media** | Delaware County Institute of Science—Minerals from around the world |
| **Patton** | Seldom Seen Mine—Tour a bituminous coal mine |
| **Philadelphia** | Academy of Natural Science—Exhibit of gems and minerals |
| | Wagner Free Institute of Science—Rocks and minerals |
| **Pittsburgh** | Carnegie Museum of Natural History—Gems and minerals |
| **Scranton** | Anthracite Museum Complex—Several anthracite coal–related attractions, including mine tours and museums |
| **Tarentum** | Tour-Ed Mine—Bituminous coal mine tour |
| **Waynesburg** | Paul R. Stewart Museum, Waynesburg College—Outstanding mineral collection |
| **West Chester** | Geology Museum, West Chester University—Specimens from Chester County, fluorescent specimens |
| **Wilkes-Barre** | Luzerne County Historical Society—Displays on anthracite coal mining |
| **Windber** | Windber Coal Heritage Center—Exhibits present the heritage of coal mining |

Annual Events

**Pittsburgh**    The Carnegie Museum of Natural History Gem & Mineral Show—
Weekend before Thanksgiving

**University Park**  Mineral Symposium—Three days in May

## RHODE ISLAND

Fee Dig Mines and Guide Services
> None

Museums and Mine Tours

**Providence**    Museum of Natural History and Planetarium—Rocks and minerals

## SOUTH CAROLINA

Fee Dig Mines and Guide Services
> None

Museums and Mine Tours

**Charleston**    Charleston Museum—Small display of gems and minerals

**Clemson**    Bob Campbell Geology Museum—Minerals, meteorites, faceted
stones

**Columbia**    McKissick Museum, University of South Carolina Campus—Exhibits
on geology and gemstones

South Carolina State Museum—Small display of rocks and minerals

## SOUTH DAKOTA

Fee Dig Mines and Guide Services

**Deadwood**    Broken Boot Gold Mine—Pan for gold

**Hill City**    Wade's Gold Mill—Pan for gold

**Keystone**    Big Thunder Gold Mine—Pan for gold

**Lead**    Black Hills Mining Museum—Pan for gold

**Wall**    Buffalo Gap National Grasslands—Hunt for agates

Museums and Mine Tours

**Deadwood**    Broken Boot Gold Mine—Gold mine tour

**Hill City**    Wade's Gold Mill—Guided tour and displays of mining equipment

**Keystone**    Big Thunder Gold Mine—Underground mine tour

**Lead**    Black Hills Mining Museum—Simulated underground mine tour

Homestead Visitors Center—Gold mining displays

| | |
|---|---|
| **Murdo** | National Rockhound and Lapidary Hall of Fame—Gems and minerals |
| **Rapid City** | South Dakota School of Mines and Technology—Local minerals |
| | Journey Museum—Geology of Black Hills |

## TENNESSEE

### Fee Dig Mines and Guide Services
| | |
|---|---|
| **Ducktown** | Burra Burra Mine—Dig for garnets, pyrite, chalcopyrite, pyrrhotite, actinolite |

### Museums and Mine Tours
| | |
|---|---|
| **Johnson City** | Hands On! Regional Museum—Simulated coal mine |
| **Knoxville** | McClung Museum—Geology of Tennessee |
| **Memphis** | Memphis Pink Palace Museum—Geology and minerals from famous mid-South localities |

## TEXAS

### Fee Dig Mines and Guide Services
| | |
|---|---|
| **Alpine** | Stillwell Ranch—Hunt for agate and jasper |
| | Woodward Ranch—Hunt for agate, precious opal, and others |
| | Seaquist Ranch—Hunt for topaz |
| **Three Rivers** | House Ranch—Hunt for agate |

### Museums and Mine Tours
| | |
|---|---|
| **Alpine** | Last Frontier Museum and Antelope Lodge—Display of rocks of west Texas |
| **Austin** | Texas Memorial Museum—Gems and minerals |
| **Canyon** | Panhandle Plains Historical Museum—Gems and minerals from the TX panhandle; meteorites |
| **Fort Stockton** | Annie Riggs Memorial Museum—Rocks and minerals of Pecos County and the Big Bend area |
| **Fritch** | Alibates Flint Quarries—View ancient flint quarries |
| **Houston** | Houston Museum of Natural Science—Displays of gem and mineral specimens |
| **Marble Falls** | Granite Mountain—View marble mining operations |
| **McKinney** | The Heard Natural Science Museum and Wildlife Sanctuary—Rocks and minerals |
| **Odessa** | Odessa Meteor Crater—Meteorite crater |

Annual Events

**Alpine**            Alpine Gem Show—Mid-April

## UTAH

Fee Dig Mines and Guide Services

**Dugaway
Mountains**          Dugaway Geode Beds—Dig for geodes
**Kanab**            Joe's Rock Shop—Dig for septarian nodules

Museums and Mine Tours

**Bingham
Canyon**             Bingham Canyon Mine Visitors Center—Overlook for open-pit-copper mine
**Eureka**           Tintec Mining Museum—Mineral display and mining artifacts
**Helper**           Western Mining and Railroad Museum—Mining exhibits, simulated 1900 coal mine
**Hyrum**            Hyrum City Museum—Display of fluorescent minerals
**Lehi**             John Hutchings Museum of Natural History—Minerals linked to mining districts, display of uncut gems
**Salt Lake City**   Utah Museum of Natural History—Mineral classification; UT ores and minerals, fluorescent minerals

## VERMONT

Fee Dig Mines and Guide Services
                     None

Museums and Mine Tours

**Barre**            Rock of Ages Corporation—Watch granite being quarried
**Norwich**          Montshire Museum of Science—Fluorescent minerals
**Proctor**          Vermont Marble Exhibit—Story of marble

## VIRGINIA

Fee Dig Mines and Guide Services

**Amelia**           Morefield Gem Mine—Dig and sluice for garnet, quartz, topaz, and many others
**Stuart**           Fairy Stone State Park—Hunt for staurolite crystals (fairy stones)
**Virginia City**    Virginia City Gem Mine—Pan for quartz, ruby, sapphire, garnet, gold

## Museums and Mine Tours

**Blocksburg**    Virginia Tech Geosciences Museum—Large display of Virginia minerals

**Goldvein**    Monroe Park—Tour a mine camp, gold panning demonstrations

**Harrisonburg**    The James Madison University Mineral Museum—Crystals, gems, fluorescent display, specimens from Amelia

**Martinsville**    Stone Cross Mountain Museum—A museum of "Fairy Crosses," specimens of staurolite

Virginia Museum of Natural History—Minerals and mining exhibits

**Pocahontas**    Pocahontas Exhibition Mine and Museum—Coal mine tour

**Richmond**    University of Richmond Museum—Displays Virginia minerals and a 2,400-carat blue topaz

## WASHINGTON

### Fee Dig Mines and Guide Services

**Olympia Baker**    Snoqualmie National Forest—Pan for gold

**Ravensdale**    Bob Jackson's Geology Adventures—Field trips: collect quartz, garnets, topaz, and others

### Museums and Mine Tours

**Castle Rock**    Mount St. Helens National Volcanic Monument—Focus on geology

**Ellensburg**    Kittitas County Historical Museum and Society—Polished rocks

**Pullman**    Washington State University—Silicified wood, minerals

**Seattle**    Burke Museum of Natural History and Culture—Rocks, minerals, the geology of Washington, and a walk-through volcano

## WEST VIRGINIA

### Fee Dig Mines and Guide Services

None

### Museums and Mine Tours

**Beckley**    The Beckley Exhibition Coal Mine—Tour a bituminous coal mine

**Charleston**    The Avampato Discovery Museum at the Clay Center—Exhibits show the story behind West Virginia's geology

**Morgantown**    Museum of Geology and Natural History—Geology of West Virginia

## WISCONSIN

### Fee Dig Mines and Guide Services

None

## Museums and Mine Tours

**Dodgeville**   The Museum of Minerals and Crystals—Local mineral specimens, specimens from around the world

**Hurley**   Iron County Historical Museum—History of area mining, also, last remaining mine head frame in Wisconsin

**Madison**   Geology Museum, University of Wisconsin at Madison—Minerals, fluorescent minerals, model of Wisconsin cave

**Milwaukee**   Milwaukee Public Museum—Displays of geological specimens
University of Wisconsin at Milwaukee—Minerals

**Platteville**   The Mining Museum—Lead and zinc mining in the upper Mississippi Valley

**Stevens Point**   Museum of Natural History—University of Wisconsin—Stevens Point rock and mineral display

## WYOMING

### Fee Dig Mines and Guide Services

**Shell**   Trapper Galloway Ranch—Dig for moss agate

### Museums and Mine Tours

**Casper**   Tate Geological Museum—Rocks and minerals, including WY jade, and fluorescent minerals

**Cheyenne**   Wyoming State Museum—Minerals of Wyoming, coal "Swamp"

**Laramie**   Geological Museum, University of Wyoming—Rocks and minerals, fluorescent minerals from WY

**Saritoga**   Saritoga Museum—Minerals from around the world, local geology

**Worland**   Washaki Museum—Geology of Big Horn Basin

### Annual Events

**Casper**   Tate Geological Museum Symposium on Wyoming Geology—June

# Index by Gems and Minerals

This index lists all the gems and minerals that can be found at fee dig mines in the U.S., and shows the city and state where the mine is located. To use the index, look up the gem or mineral you are interested in, and note the states and cities where they are located. Then go to the state and city to find the name of the mine, and information about the mine.

The following notes provide additional information:

(#)   A number in parentheses is the number of mines in that town that have that gem or mineral.

(*)   Gem or mineral is found in the state, but the mine may also add material to the ore. Check with the individual mine for confirmation.

(FT)  Field trip.

(GS)  Guide service (location listed is the location of the guide service, not necessarily the location of the gems or minerals being collected).

(I)   Mineral has been identified at the mine site but may be difficult to find.

(M)   Museum that allows collection of one specimen as a souvenir.

(MM) Micromount (a very small crystal which, when viewed under a microscope or magnifying glass, is found to be a high-quality crystal).

(O)   Available at mine but comes from other mines.

(R)   Can be found, but is rare.

(S)   Not the main gem or mineral for which the site is known.

(SA)  "Salted" or enriched gem or mineral.

(U)   Unique to the site.

(Y)   Yearly collecting event.

**Actinolite** Tennessee: Ducktown

**Agate** Arkansas: Murfreesboro (S); Iowa: Bonaporte; Montana: Helena (S); Nevada: Gerlach; New Mexico: Deming (GS); Oklahoma: Kenton (2); North Carolina: Chimney Rock (SA); Oregon: Yachats; South Dakota: Wall; Texas: Three Rivers; Virginia: Amelia

**Banded agate**  Texas: Alpine
**Fire agate**  Arizona: Safford (2)
**Iris agate**  Texas: Alpine
**Ledge agate**  Oregon: Madras
**Moss agate**  Oregon: Madras, Mitchell; Texas: Alpine (2); Wyoming: Shell
**Polka-dot jasp-agate**  Oregon: Madras
**Plume agate**  Nevada: Reno (GS); Oregon: Madras
**Pompom agate**  Texas: Alpine
**Rainbow agate**  Oregon: Madras
**Red plume agate**  Texas: Alpine

**Albite**  Maine: Albany, Poland (GS), West Paris; New Hampshire: Grafton (I); New Mexico: Dixon

**Albite** (Cleavelandite Var.)  Maine: Poland (GS)

**Amazonite**  Virginia: Amelia

**Amber**  Texas: Mason (R); Washington: Ravensdale (GS)

**Amethyst**  Arizona: Glendale; Arkansas: Murfreesboro (S); Georgia: Cleveland, Helen (SA), Jackson's Crossroads; Maine: Bethel (R), West Paris; Montana: Dillon; Nevada: Reno (GS); New Hampshire: Grafton (I), Laconia; New Mexico: Bingham; North Carolina (*): Almond, Boone (SA), Cherokee, Franklin (5), Little Switzerland, Spruce Pine (3)
**Amethyst scepters**  Arizona: Tempe
**Crystal scepters**  Nevada: Sun Valley (GS)

**Amblygonite**  Maine: West Paris

**Amphibolite**  New Hampshire: Grafton (I)

**Apatite**  Maine: Auburn, Bethel, Poland (GS), West Paris; New Hampshire: Grafton; New Mexico, Dixon
**Fluorapatite**  Maine: Poland (GS)
**Hydroxylapatite**  Maine: Poland (GS)
**Purple apatite**  Maine: West Paris

**Aplite**  New Hampshire: Grafton (I)

**Aquamarine**  California: Pala; Georgia: LaGrange; Maine: Bethel, Poland (GS); New Hampshire: Grafton (I); North Carolina (*): Boone (SA), Chimney Rock (SA), Hiddenite, Little Switzerland (2), Marion, Micaville, Spruce Pine (1) (FT)
**Brushy Creek aquamarine**  North Carolina: Spruce Pine (1) (FT)
**Weisman aquamarine**  North Carolina: Spruce Pine (1) (FT)

**Aragonite**  Arizona: Glendale (GS)

**Arsenopyrite**  Maine: Poland (GS)

**Augelite**  Maine: Poland (GS)

**Aurichalcite**  New Mexico: Bingham, Magdalena

**Autenite**  Maine: Poland (GS); New Hampshire: Grafton (I)

**Azurite** New Mexico: Magdalena; Utah: Moab (GS)

**Barite** Arizona: Glendale (GS); Arkansas: Murfreesboro (S); Georgia: Lincolnton; New Mexico: Bingham; Washington: Ravensdale (GS)

**Beraumite** Maine: Poland (GS)

**Bermanite** Maine: Poland (GS)

**Bertrandite** Maine: Poland (GS), West Paris

**Bertranite** New Hampshire: Grafton (I)

**Beryl** Georgia: LaGrange; Maine: Poland (GS), West Paris; New Mexico, Dixon; North Carolina (*): Little Switzerland (2), Spruce Pine (2); South Dakota: Custer (GS); Virginia: Amelia (2)
   **Aqua beryl** New Hampshire: Grafton (I)
   **Blue beryl** (see also aquamarine) New Hampshire: Grafton (I)
   **Golden beryl** North Carolina: Micaville (FT); New Hampshire: Grafton (I)

**Beryllonite** Maine: Poland (GS), West Paris

**Biotite** New Hampshire: Grafton (I); North Carolina: Micaville (FT)

**Borate** California: Boron (Y)

**Bornite** New Hampshire: Grafton (I)

**Brazilianite** Maine: Poland (GS)

**Brochantite** New Mexico: Bingham

**Calcite** Arizona: Glendale (GS); Arkansas: Murfreesboro (S); Florida: Ft. Drum; Michigan: Hubbell; New Hampshire: Grafton; New Mexico: Bingham; New York: Middleville; Virginia: Amelia

**Cape May "diamonds"** See Quartz

**Casserite** Maine: Poland (GS)

**Cassiterite** Maine: West Paris

**Cerussite** New Mexico: Bingham

**Chalcedony** Arizona: Safford; Nevada: Reno (GS); New Mexico: Deming

**Chalcopyrite** Tennessee: Ducktown

**Childrenite** Maine: Poland (GS)

**Chrysoberyl** Maine: West Paris; New Hampshire: Grafton (I)

**Chrysocolla** Arizona: Glendale (GS); New Mexico: Bingham

**Citrine** Georgia: Helen (SA); North Carolina (SA): Almond, Boone, Cherokee, Franklin (6), Little Switzerland, Spruce Pine (3)

**Clarkite** New Hampshire: Grafton (I)

**Clevelandite** California: Pala; Maine: Auburn, West Paris; New Hampshire: Grafton (I); New Mexico: Dixon

**Columbite** New Hampshire: Grafton (I); Maine: Bethel, Poland (GS), West Paris

**Compotite**  New Hampshire: Grafton (I)

**Cookeite**  Maine: West Paris

**Copper minerals**  Michigan: Hubbell, Mohawk (M); New Mexico: Magdalena

**Covellite**  New Mexico: Bingham

**Crandalite**  Georgia: Lincolnton

**Cryolite**  New Hampshire: Grafton (I)

**Cuprite**  New Mexico: Bingham

**Cymatolite**  New Hampshire: Grafton (I)

**Dendrites**  Nevada: Gerlach; New Hampshire: Grafton (I)

**Diadochite**  Maine: Poland (GS)

**Diamond**  Arkansas: Murfreesboro

**Dickinsonite**  Maine: Poland (GS)

**Dolomite crystals**  New York: Middleville

**Earlshannonite**  Maine: Poland (GS)

**Elbaite**  See listing under Tourmaline

**Emerald**  Georgia: Cleveland, Dahlonega (SA); North Carolina (*): Almond, Boone
(SA), Cherokee, Chimney Rock (SA), Franklin, Hiddenite, Little Switzerland (2),
Marion, Micaville (FT), Spruce Pine
    **Crabtree Emerald**  North Carolina: Spruce Pine

**Eosphorite**  Maine: Poland (GS)

**Epidote**  Michigan: Hubbell

**Fairfieldite**  Maine: Poland (GS)

**Fairy stones**  (See Staurolite crystals)

**Feldspar**  Maine: Auburn; New Hampshire: Grafton (I); North Carolina: Marion,
Micaville (FT); Virginia: Amelia
    **Albite feldspar**  Maine: Bethel

**Flint**  Ohio: Hopewell (2)

**Fluoroapatite**  New Hampshire: Grafton (I)

**Fluorescent minerals**  Arizona: Glendale (GS); New Jersey: Franklin; North Carolina:
Little Switzerland; Washington: Ravensdale (GS)

**Fluorite**  New Mexico: Bingham, Socorro (Y); South Dakota: Custer (GS); Virginia:
Amelia; Washington: Ravensdale (GS)
    **Aqua Fluorite**  Arizona: Glendale (GS)

**Franklinite**  New Jersey: Franklin

**Gahnite (spinel)**  Maine: Poland (GS), West Paris

**Gainsite**  Maine: Poland (GS)

**Galena**  Arizona: Glendale (GS); New Mexico: Bingham

**Garnets**  Arizona: Tempe; California: Pala; Connecticut: Roxbury; Georgia: Dahlonega (SA), Helen (SA); Idaho: St. Maries; Maine: Auburn, Bethel, Poland (GS), West Paris; Montana: Alder, Helena (S); New Hampshire: Grafton (I); New Mexico: Dixon; New York: North River; North Carolina (*): Almond, Boone, Canton, Cherokee, Chimney Rock, Franklin (4), Hiddenite, Highlands, Little Switzerland (2), Marion, Marshall, Spruce Pine (3) (FT); Nevada: Ely; Tennessee: Ducktown; Virginia: Virginia City (SA); Washington: Ravensdale (GS)
> **Almandine garnets**  Maine: Poland (GS); Nevada: Ely
> **Pyrope garnets**  North Carolina: Franklin
> **Rhodolite garnets**  North Carolina: Franklin (5)

**Garnets, Star**  Idaho: Moscow (GS), St. Maries; North Carolina: Micaville (FT)

**Geodes**  Arizona: Safford; Missouri: Alexandria; New Mexico: Deming; Utah: Dugaway Mountains
*Lined with:*
> **Agate, blue**  New Mexico: Deming
> **Aragonite**  Missouri: Alexandria
> **Barites**  Missouri: Alexandria
> **Chalcedony**  New Mexico: Deming
> **Dolomite**  Missouri: Alexandria
> **Goethite**  Missouri: Alexandria
> **Hematite**  Missouri: Alexandria
> **Kaoline**  Missouri: Alexandria
> **Opal, common**  New Mexico: Deming
> **Quartz**  New Mexico: Deming
> **Selenite needles**  Missouri: Alexandria
> **Sphalerite**  Missouri: Alexandria

**Gold**  (*) Alaska: Anchorage, Chugach, Copper Center, Fairbanks (3), Girdwood, McGrath, Nome, Talkeetna; Arizona: Apache Junction, Goldfield, Prescott, Wickenburg; California, Angels Camp (GS), Coloma, Columbia, Jackson, Jamestown, Mariposa, Nevada City, Pine Grove, Placerville; Colorado: Idaho Springs (2); Georgia: Cleveland, Dahlonega (2), Gainesville, Helen; Idaho: Moscow (GS); Indiana: Knightstown; Montana: Alder (O), Helena, Libby; North Carolina: Cherokee, Marion, New London (2), Stanfield, Union Mills; Oregon: Baker City, Jacksonville, Medford, Rosebury, Salem, Unity; South Dakota: Deadwood, Keystone, Lead; Virginia: Virginia City (SA); Washington: Olympia

**Gossanite**  California: Pala

**Goyazite**  Maine: Poland (GS)

**Graftonite**  Maine: Poland (GS); New Hampshire: Grafton (I)

**Granite, graphic**  Maine: Auburn

**Gummite**  New Hampshire: Grafton (I)

**Hedenburgite**  New Mexico: Magdalena

**Hematite**  Georgia: Lincolnton; Michigan: Hubbell; Montana: Helena; New Mexico: Magdalena; North Carolina: Chimney Rock (SA)

**Hemimorphite**  New Mexico: Bingham

**Herderite, hydroxyl**  Maine: Bethel, Poland (GS), West Paris

**Herkimer "diamonds"**  See Quartz

**Heterosite**  Maine: Poland (GS)

**Hiddenite (spodumene)**  North Carolina: Hiddenite

**Hureaylite**  Maine: Poland (GS)

**Iron minerals**  New Mexico: Magdalena

**Iron ore**  Michigan: Iron Mountain (M)

**Jade**  California: Pine Grove

**Jadite**  Montana: Helena (S)

**Jahnsite**  Maine: Poland (GS)

**Jasper**  Arkansas: Murfreesboro (S); California: Pine Grove; Montana: Helena (S); Oklahoma: Kenton; Oregon: Madras, Yachats; Texas: Alpine
    **Brown jasper**  New Mexico: Deming
    **Chocolate jasper**  New Mexico: Deming
    **Orange jasper**  New Mexico: Deming
    **Picture jasper**  Oregon: Mitchell
    **Pink jasper**  New Mexico: Deming
    **Variegated jasper**  New Mexico: Deming
    **Yellow jasper**  New Mexico: Deming

**Jarosite**  Georgia: Lincolnton; New Mexico: Bingham

**Kaolinite**  Maine: Poland (GS)

**Kasolite**  New Hampshire: Grafton (I)

**Kosnarite**  Maine: Poland (GS)

**Kyanite**  Georgia: Lincolnton; North Carolina (*): Franklin, Little Switzerland

**Labradorite**  Texas: Alpine

**Lake County "diamonds"**  See Quartz

**Landsite**  Maine: Poland (GS)

**Laueite**  Maine: Poland (GS)

**Lazulite**  Georgia: Lincolnton

**Lepidolite**  Maine: Poland (GS), West Paris; New Mexico: Dixon; North Carolina (*): Little Switzerland
    **Lemon Yellow Lepidolite**  New Hampshire: Grafton (I)
    **Purple Lepidolite**  California: Pala

**Lepidomelane**  New Hampshire: Grafton (I)

**Limanite**  Arizona: Tempe

**Linarite**  New Mexico: Bingham

**Lithiophyllite**  Maine: Poland (GS); New Hampshire: Grafton (I)

**Lollingite**  Maine: Poland (GS)

**Ludlamite**  Maine: Poland (GS)

**Magnesium oxide**  See Psilomellane

**Magnesium oxide minerals**  New Mexico: Deming

**Malachite**  New Mexico: Magdalena; Utah: Moab (GS)

**Manganapatite**  New Hampshire: Grafton (I)

**Manganese minerals**  New Mexico: Deming

**Manganese oxide minerals**  New Mexico: Deming

**Marcasite**  New Hampshire: Grafton (I)

**McCrillisite**  Maine: Poland (GS)

**Mica**  Maine: Poland (GS), West Paris; New Hampshire: Grafton (I), Laconia; North
  Carolina: Canton; South Dakota: Custer (GS); Virginia: Amelia
   **Book mica**  California: Pala
   **Muscovite mica**  California: Pala

**Microcline**  Maine: Poland (GS)

**Microlite**  New Mexico: Dixon

**Mitridatite**  Maine: Poland (GS)

**Molybdenite**  New Hampshire: Grafton

**Montebrasite**  Maine: Poland (GS)

**Montmorillonite**  Maine: Poland (GS), West Paris; New Hampshire: Grafton (I)

**Monzaite**  Maine: Poland (GS)

**Moonstone**  North Carolina (*): Franklin (4), Highlands, Little Switzerland, Marion,
  Micaville (FT)

**Moraesite**  Maine: Poland (GS)

**Morganite**  California: Pala

**Murdochite**  New Mexico: Bingham

**Muscovite**  Georgia: Lincolnton; New Hampshire: Grafton (I); New Mexico: Dixon

**Olivine**  North Carolina: Micaville (FT)

**Opal**
   **Black opal**  Nevada: Orovado
   **Black fire opal**  Nevada: Denio
   **Common opal**  New Mexico: Deming

**Crystal**  Nevada: Denio
**Fire opal**  Nevada: Denio, Orovado, Reno (GS); Oregon: Klamath Falls
**Hyalite opal**  Maine: Bethel
**Precious opal**  Idaho: Spencer; Texas: Alpine
**Virgin Valley**  Nevada: Reno (GS)
**White opal**  Nevada: Denio
**Wood opal**  Nevada: Denio

**Orthoclase**  Maine: Poland (GS)

**Perhamite**  Maine: Poland (GS)

**Parsonite**  New Hampshire: Grafton (I)

**Perlite (black to gray)**  New Mexico: Deming

**Peridot**  Arkansas: Murfreesboro (S); North Carolina (*): Boone (SA), Chimney Rock (SA), Franklin

**Petalite**  Maine: Poland (GS), West Paris

**Phenakite**  Virginia: Amelia

**Phosphosiderite**  Georgia: Lincolnton; Maine: Poland (GS)

**Phosphouranylite**  Maine: Poland (GS)

**Phosphyanylite**  New Hampshire: Grafton (I)

**Pitch Stone with seams of red & brown**  New Mexico: Deming

**Plattnerite**  New Mexico: Bingham

**Pollucite**  Maine: Poland (GS), West Paris

**Psilomelane**  New Hampshire: Grafton (I)

**Purpurite**  Maine: Poland (GS); New Hampshire: Grafton (I)

**Pyrite**  Georgia: Lincolnton; Maine: Bethel, Poland (GS); New Hampshire: Grafton (I); New Mexico: Magdalena; Tennessee: Ducktown; Virginia: Amelia, Virginia City (SA); Washington: Ravensdale (GS)

**Pyrophyllite**  Georgia: Lincolnton

**Pyrrhotite**  New Hampshire: Grafton (I); Tennessee: Ducktown

**Quartz**  Arizona: Glendale (GS), Tempe; Arkansas: Hot Springs, Jessieville (2), Mt. Ida (6) (Y), Murfreesboro (S), Pencil Bluff; California: Pine Grove; Colorado: Lake George; Georgia: Lincolnton; Maine: Poland (GS); Montana: Dillon, Helena (S); New Hampshire: Grafton, Laconia; New Mexico: Bingham, Deming, Dixon, Socorro (Y); North Carolina: Chimney Rock; Pennsylvania: Williamsport; Texas: Alpine; Virginia: Amelia, Virginia City (SA); Washington: Ravensdale (GS)

**Blue**  Georgia: Lincolnton; North Carolina: Marion
**Clear**  North Carolina (*): Franklin, Hiddenite, Little Switzerland, Marion, Spruce Pine
**Milky**  Maine: Bethel
**Parallel growth**  Maine: West Paris

**Pseudocubic crystals**  Maine: West Paris

**Rose**  Georgia: Helen (SA); Maine: Auburn; New Hampshire: Grafton (I); North Carolina (*): Franklin, Little Switzerland, Marion

**Rose (gem quality)**  Maine: West Paris

**Rutilated**  North Carolina (*): Little Switzerland, Spruce Pine

**Smoky**  Georgia: Helen (SA); Maine: Bethel; Nevada: Reno (GS); New Hampshire: Grafton (I); North Carolina (*): Almond, Boone (SA), Cherokee, Franklin (5), Hiddenite, Highlands, Little Switzerland (2), Marion, Spruce Pine (2)

**Smoky (gem quality)**  Maine: West Paris

**Stone Rose**  Georgia: LaGrange

## Quartz "diamonds"

**Lake Co. "diamonds" (moon tears)**  California: Lake County

**Cape May "diamonds"**  New Jersey: Cape May

**Herkimer "diamonds"**  New York: Herkimer, Middleville, St. Johnsville

**Reddingite**  Maine: Poland (GS); New Hampshire: Grafton (I)

**Rhodochrosite**  Maine: Poland (GS)

**Rhodolite (garnet)**  North Carolina: Franklin (1)

**Rochbridgeite**  Maine: Poland (GS)

**Rose rocks**  See Barite Rose

**Rubies**  California: Pine Grove; Georgia: Cleveland, Dahlonega (SA); Montana: Helena (R); North Carolina (*): Almond, Boone (SA); Cherokee, Franklin (10), Highlands, Little Switzerland (2), Spruce Pine (3); Virginia: Virginia City (SA)

**Rutile**  Georgia: Lincolnton; Maine: Bethel, Poland (GS); North Carolina: Franklin (1), Hiddenite; Virginia: Amelia

**Safflorite**  New Hampshire: Grafton (I)

**Sapphires**  Georgia: Cleveland, Dahlonega (SA); Montana: Alder (O), Clinton (GS), Gem Mountain, Hamilton, Helena (2), Philipsburg; North Carolina (*): Almond, Canton, Cherokee, Franklin (10), Hiddenite, Highlands, Little Switzerland (2), Spruce Pine; Virginia: Virginia City (SA)

**Star Sapphire**  North Carolina: Boone (SA)

**Scheelite**  Maine: West Paris

**Selenite crystals**  New Mexico: Bingham; Oklahoma: Jet (Y)

**Septarian nodules**  Utah: Kanab

**Serpentine**  Montana: Helena (S)

**Siderite**  Maine: Bethel

**Silica minerals**  New Mexico: Deming

**Sillimanite**  New Hampshire: Grafton (I); North Carolina (*): Franklin (1), Hiddenite

**Silver**  Michigan: Hubbell

**Smithsonite**  Arizona: Glendale (GS); New Mexico: Bingham, Magdalena, Socorro (Y)

**Sodalite**  North Carolina: Chimney Rock (SA)

**Spangolite**  New Mexico: Bingham

**Spessartine**  New Mexico: Dixon

**Spodumene**  Maine: Poland (GS), West Paris; New Mexico: Dixon
    **Altered Spodumene**  Maine: West Paris
    **Hiddenite**  North Carolina: Hiddenite

**Staurolite**  New Hampshire: Grafton (I); Virginia: Stuart

**Stewartite**  Maine: Poland (GS)

**Strengite**  Georgia: Lincolnton

**Strunzite**  Maine: Poland (GS)

**Sulfur**  Georgia: Lincolnton

**Sunstones**  Nevada: Reno (GS); Oregon: Plush

**Switzerite**  Maine: Poland (GS)

**Tantalite-Columbite**  New Mexico: Dixon; Virginia: Amelia

**Thulite**  North Carolina: Micaville (FT)

**Thundereggs**  New Mexico: Deming; Oregon: Madras, Mitchell

**Tobernite**  New Hampshire: Grafton (I)

**Topaz**  Georgia: Cleveland, Helen (SA); Maine: Poland (GS); Montana: Helena (R); New Hampshire: Grafton (I); North Carolina (SA): Almond, Boone, Cherokee, Franklin (5), Little Switzerland (3), Spruce Pine (3); Texas: Mason; Virginia: Amelia
    **Phenakite crystals in topaz**  Colorado
    **Pink topaz**  Washington: Ravensdale (GS)

**Torberite**  Maine: Poland (GS)

**Tourmaline**  Arizona: Tempe; California: Mesa Grande; Maine: Auburn (2), Poland (GS), West Paris; North Carolina (*): Boone (SA) Franklin (6), Hiddenite, Highlands, Little Switzerland (3), Spruce Pine (3) (FT); Virginia: Amelia
    **Bi-colored**  California: Pala
    **Black tourmaline**  California: Pala; Georgia: LaGrange; Maine: Auburn, Bethel, Poland (GS), West Paris; New Hampshire: Grafton (I); North Carolina: Micaville (FT)
    **Gem tourmaline**  Maine: West Paris
    **Green tourmaline**  California: Pala; Maine: West Paris
    **Pink tourmaline**  California: Pala

**Triphyllite**  Maine: Poland (GS), West Paris; New Hampshire: Grafton (I)

**Triplite**  Maine: Poland (GS)

**Turquoise**  Nevada: Reno (GS)

**Uralolite**  Maine: Poland (GS)

**Uranite**  Maine: Poland (GS); New Hampshire: Grafton (I) (Species with gummite—world-famous)

**Uranium minerals**  New Hampshire: Grafton (I)

**Uranophane**  New Hampshire: Grafton (I)

**Vandendriesscheite**  New Hampshire: Grafton (I)

**Variscite**  Georgia: Lincolnton; Nevada: Reno (GS)

**Vesuvianite**  Maine: Poland (GS), West Paris (1)

**Vivianite**  New Hampshire: Grafton (I)

**Voelerkenite**  New Hampshire: Grafton (I)

**Wardilite**  Maine: Poland (GS)

**Whitlockite**  Maine: Poland (GS)

**Whitmoreite**  Maine: Poland (GS)

**Willemite**  Arizona: Glendale (GS)

**Wodginite**  Maine: Poland (GS)

**Wulfenite**  Arizona: Glendale (GS); New Mexico: Bingham

**Zircon**  Maine: Bethel, Poland (GS), West Paris; New Hampshire: Grafton (I); North Carolina: Canton

# Annual Events

## JANUARY

Quartzite, AZ, Gem and Mineral Shows—Mid-January–mid-February

## FEBRUARY

Tucson, AZ, Gem and Mineral Show—First two weeks in February

## MARCH

Scottsdale, AZ, Minerals of Arizona Symposium—1 day in March each year, sponsored by the Arizona Mineral & Mining Museum Foundation and the Arizona Department of Mines & Mineral Resources

Boron, CA, Rock Bonanza—Weekend before Easter

## APRIL

Alpine, TX, Alpine Gem Show—Mid-April

## MAY

Cherokee, OK, The Crystal Festival and Selenite Crystal Dig—First Saturday in May

Augusta, ME, Maine Mineral Symposium—Third weekend in May

Poland, ME, Maine Pegmatite Workshop—End of May

## JUNE

Prineville, OR, Rockhounds Pow-Wow—Mid-June

Casper, WY, Tate Geological Museum Symposium on Wyoming Geology

## JULY

**Franklin, NC,** Macon County Gemboree—Third weekend in July

**Cottage Grove, OR,** Bohemia Mining Days—Four days in July

## AUGUST

**Spruce Pine, NC,** Original North Carolina Mineral and Gem Festival—Four days at the beginning of August

**Pittsburgh, PA,** Carnegie Museum of Natural History Gem and Mineral Show—Last weekend in August

## SEPTEMBER

No information available.

## OCTOBER

**Coloma, CA,** Marshall Gold Discovery State Park Gold Rush Days—End of September–beginning of October

**Dahlonega, GA,** Gold Rush Days—Third weekend in October

**Jasper, GA,** Pickens County Marble Festival—First weekend in October

**Mt. Ida, AR,** Quartz Crystal Festival and World Championship Dig—Second weekend in October

**Franklin, NC,** "Leaf Looker" Gemboree—Second weekend in October

## NOVEMBER

**Socorro, NM,** New Mexico Mineral Symposium—Two days in November

## DECEMBER

No information available.

# State Gem and Mineral Symbols

| STATE | GEMSTONE | MINERAL | STONE/ROCK |
|---|---|---|---|
| Alabama | Star Blue Quartz (1990) | Hematite (1967) | Marble (1969) |
| Alaska | Jade (1968) | Gold (1968) | |
| Arizona | Turquoise (1974) | Fire agate | Petrified Wood |
| Arkansas | Diamond | Quartz crystal | Bauxite |
| California | Benitoite | Gold | Serpentine (1965) |
| Colorado | Aquamarine (1971) | Rhodochrosite | |
| Connecticut | Garnet (1977) | | |
| Delaware | | | Sillimanite |
| Florida | Moonstone | | Agatized coral |
| Georgia | Quartz | Staurolite | |
| Hawaii | Black Coral | | |
| Idaho | Star Garnet (1967) | | |
| Illinois | | Fluorite (1965) | |
| Indiana | | | Limestone |
| Iowa | | | Geode |
| Kansas | | | |
| Kentucky | Freshwater Pearl | Coal | Kentucky Agate |
| Louisiana | Agate | | Petrified Palm |
| Maine | Tourmaline (1971) | | |
| Maryland | | Patuxent River Stone | |
| Massachusetts | Rhodonite | Babingtonite | Plymouth Rock, Dighton Rock, Roxbury Conglomerate |
| Michigan | Isle Royal Greenstone (Chlorostrolite) (1972) | | Petosky Stone (1965) |
| Minnesota | Lake Superior Agate | | |
| Mississippi | | | Petrified Wood (1976) |
| Missouri | | Galena (1967) | Mozarkite (1967) |

| STATE | GEMSTONE | MINERAL | STONE/ROCK |
|---|---|---|---|
| Montana | Yogo Sapphire & Agate (1969) | | |
| Nebraska | Blue Agate (1967) | | Prairie Agate (1967) |
| Nevada | Virgin Valley Blackfire Opal (1987) (Precious) Turquoise (1987) (Semiprecious) | Silver (Official Metal) | Sandstone (1987) |
| New Hampshire | Smoky Quartz | Beryl | Granite |
| New Jersey | | | Stockton Sandstone |
| New Mexico | Turquoise (1967) | | |
| New York | Garnet (1969) | | |
| North Carolina | Emerald (1973) | | Granite/Unakite |
| North Dakota | | | Teredo Wood |
| Ohio | Flint (1965) | | |
| Oklahoma | | | Barite Rose |
| Oregon | Sunstone (1987) | | Thundereggs (1965) |
| Pennsylvania | | | Trilobite |
| Rhode Island | | Bowenite | Cumberlandite |
| South Carolina | Amethyst | | Blue Granite |
| South Dakota | Fairburn Agate (1966) | Rose Quartz (1966) (Mineral/Stone) | |
| Tennessee | Tennessee River Pearls | Tennessee Limestone and Agate | |
| Texas | Texas Blue Topaz (1969) Lone Star Cut (1977) (Gemstone Cut) | | Petrified Palmwood (1960) |
| Utah | Topaz | Copper | Coal |
| Vermont | Grossular Garnet | Talc | Granite, Marble, Slate |
| Virginia | | | |
| Washington | Petrified Wood (1975) | | |
| West Virginia | Mississippian Coral, Lithostrotionella | | |
| Wisconsin | Ruby | Galena (1971) | Wausau Red Granite (1971) |
| Wyoming | Nephrite Jade (1967) | | |

# Finding Your Own Birthstone

Following is a listing of fee dig sites presented in this four-volume guide where you can find your birthstone! Refer to the individual mine listings for more information on individual mines.

**Garnet (January Birthstone)** Arizona: Tempe; California: Pala; Connecticut: Roxbury; Georgia: Dahlonega (SA), Helen (SA); Idaho: St. Maries; Maine: Auburn, Bethel, Poland (GS), West Paris; Montana: Alder, Helena (S); Nevada: Reno (GS); New Hampshire: Grafton (I); New Mexico: Dixon; New York: North River; North Carolina (*): Almond, Boone (SA), Cherokee, Chimney Rock (SA), Franklin (5), Hiddenite, Highlands, Little Switzerland (2), Marshall, Spruce Pine (3) (FT); Nevada: Ely; Virginia: Virginia City (SA); Washington: Ravensdale (GS)
> **Almandine garnets** Maine: Poland (GS); Nevada: Ely
> **Pyrope garnets** North Carolina: Franklin
> **Rhodolite garnets** North Carolina: Franklin (5)

**Amethyst (February Birthstone)** Arizona: Glendale (GS); Arkansas: Murfreesboro(S); Georgia: Cleveland, Helen (SA), Jackson's Crossroads; Maine: Bethel (R), West Paris; Montana: Dillon; Nevada: Reno (GS), Sun Valley (GS) (crystal scepters); New Hampshire: Grafton (I), Laconia; New Mexico: Bingham; North Carolina (*): Almond, Boone (SA), Cherokee, Chimney Rock (SA), Franklin (4), Highlands, Little Switzerland, Spruce Pine (3)
> **Amethyst scepters** Arizona: Tempe

**Aquamarine or Bloodstone (March Birthstone):**
> **Aquamarine** Georgia: LaGrange; Maine: Bethel, Poland (GS); New Hampshire: Grafton (I); North Carolina (*): Boone (SA), Chimney Rock (SA), Hiddenite, Little Switzerland (5), Marion, Micaville (FT), Spruce Pine (1) (FT)
> **Brushy Creek Aq.** North Carolina: Spruce Pine (FT)
> **Weisman Aq.** North Carolina: Spruce Pine (FT)
> **Bloodstone** No listing

**Diamond (April Birthstone)** Arkansas: Murfreesboro

**Emerald (May Birthstone)** Georgia: Cleveland, Dahlonega (SA); North Carolina (*): Boone (SA), Cherokee, Chimney Rock (SA), Franklin, Hiddenite, Little Switzerland (2), Marion, Micaville, Spruce Pine (1)
> **Crabtree Emerald** North Carolina: Spruce Pine

**Moonstone or Pearl (June Birthstone):**
**Moonstone** North Carolina (*): Franklin (6), Little Switzerland, Marion, Spruce Pine
**Pearl** No listing

**Ruby (July Birthstone)** Georgia: Cleveland, Dahlonega (SA); Montana: Helena (R); North Carolina (*): Boone (SA), Cherokee, Chimney Rock (SA), Franklin (11), Highlands, Little Switzerland (2), Spruce Pine (3); Virginia: Virginia City (SA)

**Peridot or Sardonyx (August Birthstone):**
**Peridot** Arkansas: Murfreesboro (S); North Carolina (*): Franklin
**Sardonyx** No listing

**Sapphire (September Birthstone)** Georgia: Dahlonega (SA); Montana: Alder (O), Clinton (GS), Gem Mountian, Hamilton, Helena (2), Philipsburg; North Carolina (*): Boone (SA) Canton, Cherokee, Franklin (13), Hiddenite, Highlands, Little Switzerland (2), Spruce Pine; Virginia: Virginia City (SA)

**Opal or Tourmaline (October Birthstone):**
**Opal**
    **Black opal** Nevada: Orovado
    **Black fire opal** Nevada: Denio
    **Common opal** New Mexico: Deming
    **Crystal opal** Nevada: Denio
    **Fire opal** Nevada: Orovado, Reno (GS); Oregon: Klamath Falls
    **Hyalite opal** Maine: Bethel
    **Precious opal** Idaho: Spencer; Texas: Alpine
    **Virgin Valley** Nevada: Reno (GS)
    **White opal** Nevada: Denio
    **Wood opal** Nevada: Denio
**Tourmaline** Arizona: Tempe; California: Mesa Grande; Maine: Auburn (2), Poland (GS), West Paris; North Carolina (*): Boone (SA), Franklin (6), Hiddenite, Highlands, Little Switzerland (3), Micaville (FT), Spruce Pine (2) (FT); Virginia: Amelia
    **Black tourmaline** California: Pala; Georgia: LaGrange; Maine: Auburn, Bethel, Poland (GS), West Paris; New Hampshire: Grafton (I)
    **Gem tourmaline** Maine: West Paris
    **Green tourmaline** California: Pala; Maine: West Paris
    **Pink tourmaline** California: Pala

**Topaz (November Birthstone)** Georgia: Cleveland, Helen (SA); Maine: Poland (GS); Montana: Helena (R); New Hampshire: Grafton (I); North Carolina (SA): Cherokee, Chimney Rock (SA), Franklin (6), Little Switzerland (3), Spruce Pine (3); Texas: Mason (2); Virginia: Amelia
    **Pink topaz** Washington: Ravensdale (GS)

**Turquoise or Lapis Lazuli (December Birthstone):**
**Turquoise** Nevada: Reno (GS)
**Lapis Lazuli** No listing

The preceding list of birthstones is taken from a list adopted in 1912 by the American National Association of Jewelers ("The Evolution of Birthstones" from *Jewelry & Gems—The Buying Guide* by Antoinette Matlins and A. C. Bonanno; Gemstone Press, 2005).

# Finding Your Anniversary Stone

The following is a listing of fee dig sites contained in this four-volume guide where you can find the stone that is associated with a particular anniversary.

**First: Gold (Jewelry)** Alaska: Anchorage, Chugach, Fairbanks (3), Girdwood, McGrath, Nome, Talkeetna, Wrangell; Arizona: Goldfield, Prescott, Wickenburg; California: Angels Camp (GS), Coloma, Columbia, Jackson, Jamestown, Mariposa, Nevada City, Pine Grove, Placerville; Colorado: Idaho Springs (2); Georgia: Cleveland, Dahlonega (2), Helen; Idaho: Moscow (GS); Indiana: Knightstown; Montana: Alder (O), Helena, Libby; North Carolina: Cherokee, Marion, New London, Stanfield, Union Mills; Oregon: Baker City, Jacksonville, Medford, Rosebury, Salem, Unity; South Dakota: Deadwood, Keystone, Lead; Virginia: Virginia City (SA); Washington: Olympia

**Second: Garnet** Arizona: Tempe; California: Pala; Connecticut: Roxbury; Georgia: Dahlonega (SA), Helen (SA); Idaho: St. Maries; Maine: Auburn, Bethel, Poland (GS), West Paris; Montana: Alder, Helena (S); New Hampshire: Grafton (I); New Mexico: Dixon; New York: North River; North Carolina (*): Almond, Boone (SA), Cherokee, Chimney Rock (SA), Franklin (5), Hiddenite, Highlands, Little Switzerland (2), Marshall, Spruce Pine (3) (FT); Nevada: Ely; Virginia: Virginia City (SA); Washington: Ravensdale (GS)
    **Almandine garnets** Maine: Poland (GS); Nevada: Ely
    **Pyrope garnets** North Carolina: Franklin
    **Rhodolite garnets** North Carolina: Franklin (5)

**Third: Pearl** No listing

**Fourth: Blue Topaz** No listing

**Fifth: Sapphire** Georgia: Cleveland, Dahlonega (SA); Montana: Alder (O), Clinton (GS), Gem Mountain, Hamilton, Helena (2), Philipsburg; North Carolina (*): Almond, Boone (SA), Canton, Cherokee, Franklin (12), Hiddenite, Little Switzerland (2), Spruce Pine; Virginia: Virginia City (SA)

**Sixth: Amethyst** Arizona: Glendale (GS); Arkansas: Murfreesboro (S); Georgia: Cleveland, Helen (SA); Maine: Bethel (R), West Paris; Montana: Dillon; Nevada: Reno (GS), Sun Valley (GS) (crystal scepters); New Hampshire: Grafton (I), Laconia; New Mexico: Bingham; North Carolina (*): Boone (SA), Cherokee, Chimney Rock (SA), Franklin (4), Highlands, Little Switzerland, Spruce Pine (3)
    **Amethyst sceptors** Arizona: Tempe

**Seventh: Onyx**  No listing

**Eighth: Tourmaline**  Arizona: Tempe; California: Mesa Grande; Maine: Auburn (2), Poland (GS), West Paris; North Carolina (*): Chimney Rock (SA), Franklin (6), Hiddenite, Highlands, Little Switzerland (3), Spruce Pine (3) (FT); Virginia: Amelia

  **Black tourmaline**  California: Pala; Maine: Auburn, Bethel, Poland (GS), West Paris; New Hampshire: Grafton (I)

  **Gem tourmaline**  Maine: West Paris

  **Green tourmaline**  California: Pala; Maine: West Paris

  **Pink tourmaline**  California: Pala

**Ninth: Lapis Lazuli**  No listing

**Tenth: Diamond (Jewelry)**  Arkansas: Murfreesboro

**Eleventh: Turquoise**  Nevada: Reno

**Twelfth: Jade**  No listing

**Thirteenth: Citrine**  Georgia: Helen (SA); North Carolina (SA): Almond, Cherokee, Franklin (5), Little Switzerland, Spruce Pine (3)

**Fourteenth: Opal**

  **Black opal**  Nevada: Orovado

  **Common opal**  New Mexico: Deming

  **Fire opal**  Nevada: Orovado, Reno (GS); Oregon: Klamath Falls

  **Hyalite opal**  Maine: Bethel

  **Precious opal**  Idaho: Spencer; Texas: Alpine

  **Virgin Valley**  Nevada: Reno (GS)

  **Wood opal**  Nevada: Denio

**Fifteenth: Ruby**  California: Pine Grove; Georgia: Cleveland, Dahlonega (SA); Montana: Helena (R); North Carolina (*): Almond, Boone (SA), Cherokee, Chimney Rock (SA), Franklin (12), Highlands, Little Switzerland (2), Spruce Pine (3); Virginia: Virginia City (SA)

**Twentieth: Emerald**  Georgia: Cleveland, Dahlonega (SA); North Carolina (*): Almond, Boone (SA), Cherokee, Chimney Rock, Franklin (1), Hiddenite, Little Switzerland (4), Marion, Micaville (FT), Spruce Pine (1) (also crabtree emerald)

**Twenty-fifth: Silver**  Michigan: Hubbell

**Thirtieth: Pearl**  No listing

**Thirty-fifth: Emerald**  Georgia: Cleveland, Dahlonega (SA); North Carolina (*): Almond, Boone (SA), Cherokee, Chimney Rock (SA), Franklin, Hiddenite, Little Switzerland (2), Marion, Micaville (FT), Spruce Pine (1) (also crabree emerald)

**Fortieth: Ruby**  California: Pine Grove; Georgia: Cleveland, Dahlonega (SA); Montana: Helena (R); North Carolina (*): Almond, Boone (SA), Cherokee, Chimney Rock (SA), Franklin (12), Highlands, Little Switzerland (2), Spruce Pine (3)

**Forty-fifth: Sapphire**  Georgia: Cleveland, Dahlonega (SA); Montana: Alder, Clinton

(GS), Gem Mountain, Hamilton, Helena (2), Philipsburg; North Carolina (*): Almond, Boone (SA), Canton, Cherokee, Chimney Rock (SA), Franklin (11), Hiddenite, Highlands, Little Switzerland (2), Spruce Pine; Virginia: Viginia City (SA)

**Fiftieth: Gold** Alaska: Fairbanks (3); Arizona: Apache Junction, Goldfield, Prescott, Wickenburg; California: Angels Camp, Coloma, Columbia, Jackson, Jamestown, Mariposa, Nevada City, Pine Grove, Placerville; Colorado: Idaho Springs (2); Georgia: Cleveland, Dahlonega (2), Gainesville, Helen; Idaho: Moscow (GS); Indiana: Knightstown; Montana: Alder (O), Helena; North Carolina: Cherokee, Marion, New London, Stanfield, Union Mills; South Dakota: Deadwood, Keystone, Lead; Virginia: Virginia City (SA)

**Fifty-fifth: Alexandrite** No listing

**Sixtieth: Diamond** Arkansas: Murfreesboro

# Finding Your Zodiac Stone

The following is a listing of fee dig sites contained in this four-volume guide where you can find the stone that is associated with a particular zodiac sign. Refer to the individual mine listings for more information.

**Aquarius (January 21–February 21) Garnet**  Arizona: Tempe; California: Pala; Connecticut: Roxbury; Georgia: Dahlonega (SA), Helen (SA); Idaho: St. Maries; Maine: Auburn, Bethel, Poland (GS), West Paris; Montana: Alder, Helena (S); New Hampshire: Grafton (I); New Mexico: Dixon; New York: North River; North Carolina (*): Almond, Boone (SA), Cherokee, Chimney Rock (SA), Franklin (6), Hiddenite, Highlands, Little Switzerland (2), Marshall, Spruce Pine (3) (FT); Nevada: Ely; Virginia: Virginia City (SA); Washington: Ravensdale (GS)
> **Almandine garnets**  Maine: Poland (GS); Nevada: Ely
> **Pyrope garnets**  North Carolina: Franklin
> **Rhodolite garnets**  North Carolina: Franklin (5)

**Pisces (February 22–March 21) Amethyst**  Arizona: Glendale (GS); Arkansas: Murfreesboro (S); Georgia: Cleveland, Helen (SA), Jackson's Crossroads; Maine: Albany, Bethel (R), West Paris; Montana: Dillon; Nevada: Reno (GS), Sun Valley (GS) (crystal scepters); New Hampshire: Grafton (I), Laconia; New Mexico: Bingham; New York: North River; North Carolina (*): Almond, Boone (SA), Cherokee, Chimney Rock (SA), Franklin (4), Highlands, Little Switzerland, Marion, Spruce Pine (3)
> **Amethyst sceptors**  Arizona: Tempe

**Aries (March 21–April 20) Bloodstone** (green chalcedony with red spots)  No listing

**Taurus (April 21–May 21) Sapphire**  Georgia: Cleveland, Dahlonega (SA); Montana: Alder (O), Clinton (GS), Gem Mountain, Hamilton, Helena (2), Philipsburg; North Carolina (*): Almond, Boone (SA), Canton, Cherokee, Chimney Rock, Franklin (11), Hiddenite, Highlands, Little Switzerland (2), Spruce Pine; Virginia: Virginia City (SA)

**Gemini (May 22–June 21) Agate**  Arkansas: Murfreesboro(S); Iowa: Bonaporte; Montana: Helena (S); Nevada: Gerlach; New Mexico: Deming (GS); North Carolina: Chimney Rock (SA); Oklahoma: Kenton (2); Oregon: Yachats; South Dakota: Wall; Texas: Three Rivers; Virginia: Amelia
> **Banded agate**  Texas: Alpine
> **Fire agate**  Arizona: Safford (2)
> **Iris agate**  Texas: Alpine

**Ledge agate**  Oregon: Madras
**Moss agate**  Oregon: Madras, Mitchell; Texas: Alpine (2), Wyoming: Shell
**Polka-dot jasp-agate**  Oregon: Madras
**Plume agate**  Nevada: Reno (GS); Oregon: Madras
**Pompom agate**  Texas: Alpine
**Rainbow agate**  Oregon: Madras
**Red plume agate**  Texas: Alpine

**Cancer (June 22–July 22) Emerald**  Georgia: Cleveland, Dahlonega (SA); North Carolina (*): Almond, Boone (SA), Cherokee, Chimney Rock (SA), Franklin, Hiddenite, Little Switzerland (2), Micaville (FT), Spruce Pine (1)
    **Crabtree emerald**  North Carolina: Spruce Pine

**Leo (July 23–August 22) Onyx**  No listing

**Virgo (August 23–September 22) Carnelian**  No listing

**Libra (September 23–October 23) Chrysolite or Peridot:**
    **Peridot**  Arkansas: Murfreesboro (S); North Carolina (*): Franklin

**Scorpio (October 24–November 21) Beryl**  Georgia: LaGrange; Maine: Poland (GS), West Paris; New Mexico: Dixon; North Carolina (*): Little Switzerland (2), Spruce Pine (2); Virginia: Amelia (2)
    **Aqua beryl**  New Hampshire: Grafton (I)
    **Blue beryl**  New Hampshire: Grafton (I)
    **Clear beryl**  California: Pala
    **Golden beryl**  North Carolina: Spruce Pine (FT); New Hampshire: Grafton (I)

**Sagittarius (November 22–December 21) Topaz**  Georgia: Cleveland, Helen (SA); Maine: Poland (GS); Montana: Helena (R); New Hampshire: Grafton (I); North Carolina (SA): Boone (SA), Cherokee, Franklin (5), Highlands, Little Switzerland (3), Spruce Pine (3); Texas: Mason; Virginia: Amelia
    **Pink topaz**  Washington: Ravensdale (GS)

**Capricorn (December 22–January 21) Ruby**  California: Pine Grove; Georgia: Cleveland, Dahlonega (SA); Montana: Helena (R); North Carolina (*): Almond, Boone (SA), Cherokee, Chimney Rock (SA), Franklin (12), Highlands, Little Switzerland (2), Spruce Pine (3); Virginia: Virginia City (SA)

The preceding list of zodiacal stones has been passed on from an early Hindu legend (taken from *Jewelry & Gems—The Buying Guide* by Antoinette Matlins and A. C. Bonanno, Gemstone Press, 2005).

The following is an old Spanish list, probably representing Arab traditions, which ascribes the following stones to various signs of the zodiac (taken from *Jewelry & Gems—The Buying Guide* by Antoinette Matlins and A. C. Bonanno, Gemstone Press, 2005).

**Aquarius (January 21–February 21) Amethyst**   Arizona: Glendale (GS); Arkansas: Murfreesboro (S); Georgia: Cleveland, Helen (SA); Maine: Bethel (R), West Paris; Montana: Dillon; Nevada: Reno (GS); New Hampshire: Grafton (I), Laconia; New Mexico: Bingham; North Carolina (*): Almond, Boone (SA), Cherokee, Chimney Rock (SA), Franklin (4), Highlands, Little Switzerland, Marion, Spruce Pine (3)
   **Crystal scepters**   Nevada: Sun Valley (GS)
   **Amethyst scepters**   Arizona: Tempe

**Pisces (February 22–March 21) Undistinguishable**

**Aries (March 21–April 20) Quartz**   Arizona: Glenale (GS), Tempe; Arkansas: Hot Springs, Jessieville (2), Mt. Ida (6) (Y), Murfreesboro (S), Pencil Bluff; California: Pine Grove; Colorado: Lake George; Maine: Poland (GS); Montana: Dillon, Helena; New Hampshire: Grafton; New Mexico: Bingham, Deming, Dixon, Socorro (Y); Pennsylvania: Williamsport; Texas: Alpine; Virginia: Amelia, Virginia City (SA); Washington: Ravensdale (GS)
   **Blue**   Georgia: Lincolnton; North Carolina: Marion
   **Clear**   North Carolina (*): Franklin, Hiddenite, Little Switzerland, Marion, Spruce Pine
   **Milky**   Maine: Bethel
   **Orange**   Maine: West Paris
   **Parallel growth**   Maine: West Paris
   **Pseudocubic crystals**   Maine: West Paris
   **Rose**   Georgia: Helen (SA); New Hampshire: Grafton (I); North Carolina (*): Franklin, Little Switzerland, Marion
   **Rose (gem quality)**   Maine: Albany, West Paris
   **Rutilated**   North Carolina (*): Little Switzerland, Spruce Pine
   **Smoky**   Georgia: Helen (SA); Maine: Bethel, West Paris; New Hampshire: Grafton (I); North Carolina (*): Almond, Boone (SA), Cherokee, Franklin (5), Hiddenite, Highlands, Little Switzerland (2), Marion, Spruce Pine (2)
   **Smoky (gem quality)**   Maine: West Paris
   **Star rose**   Georgia: LaGrange

**Quartz "diamonds"**
   **Lake Co. "diamonds" (moon tears)**   California: Lake County
   **Cape May "diamonds"**   New Jersey: Cape May
   **Herkimer "diamonds"**   New York: Herkimer, Little Falls, Middleville, St. Johnsville

**Taurus (April 21–May 21) Rubies, Diamonds:**
   **Rubies**   California: Pine Grove; Georgia: Dahlonega (SA); Montana: Helena (R); North Carolina (*): Almond, Cherokee, Franklin (11), Highlands, Little Switzerland (2), Spruce Pine (3)
   **Diamonds**   Arkansas: Murfreesboro

**Gemini (May 22–June 21) Sapphire**   Georgia: Cleveland, Dahlonega (SA); Montana: Alder (O), Clinton (GS), Gem Mountain, Hamilton, Helena (2), Philipsburg; North Carolina (*): Almond, Boone (SA), Canton, Cherokee, Franklin (11), Hiddenite, Highlands, Little Switzerland (2), Spruce Pine; Virginia: Virginia City (SA)

**Cancer (June 22–July 22) Agate and Beryl:**

**Agate**  Arkansas: Murfreesboro (S); Iowa: Bonaporte; Montana: Helena (S); Nevada: Gerlach; New Mexico: Deming (GS); North Carolina: Boone (SA); Oklahoma: Kenton (2); Oregon: Yachats; South Dakota: Wall; Texas: Three Rivers; Virginia: Amelia

  **Banded agate**  Texas: Alpine
  **Fire agate**  Arizona: Safford (2)
  **Iris agate**  Texas: Alpine
  **Ledge agate**  Oregon: Madras
  **Moss agate**  Oregon: Madras, Mitchell; Texas: Alpine (2), Wyoming: Shell
  **Polka-dot agate**  Oregon: Madras (R)
  **Plume agate**  Nevada: Reno (GS); Oregon: Madras
  **Pompom agate**  Texas: Alpine
  **Rainbow agate**  Oregon: Madras (R)
  **Red plume agate**  Texas: Alpine

**Beryl**  Georgia: LaGrange; Maine: Poland (GS), West Paris; New Mexico, Dixon; North Carolina (*): Little Switzerland (2), Spruce Pine (2); Virginia: Amelia (2)

  **Aqua beryl**  New Hampshire: Grafton (I)
  **Blue beryl**  New Hampshire: Grafton (I)
  **Clear beryl**  California: Pala
  **Golden beryl**  North Carolina: Spruce Pine (FT); New Hampshire: Grafton (I)

**Leo (July 23–August 22) Topaz**  Georgia: Cleveland, Helen (SA); Maine: Poland (GS); Montana: Helena (R); New Hampshire: Grafton (I); North Carolina (SA): Boone (SA), Cherokee, Franklin (5), Highlands, Little Switzerland (3), Spruce Pine (3); Texas: Mason; Virginia: Amelia

  **Pink topaz**  Washington: Ravensdale (GS)

**Virgo (August 23–September 22) Bloodstone** (green chalcedony with red spots)
  No listing

**Libra (September 23–October 23) Jasper**  Arkansas: Murfreesboro (S); California: Pine Grove; Montana: Helena; Oklahoma: Kenton; Oregon: Madras, Yachats; Texas: Alpine

  **Brown jasper**  New Mexico: Deming
  **Chocolate jasper**  New Mexico: Deming
  **Orange jasper**  New Mexico: Deming
  **Picture jasper**  Oregon: Mitchell
  **Pink jasper**  New Mexico: Deming
  **Variegated jasper**  New Mexico: Deming
  **Yellow jasper**  New Mexico: Deming

**Scorpio (October 24–November 21) Garnet**  Arizona: Tempe; California: Pala; Connecticut: Roxbury; Georgia: Dahlonega (SA), Helen (SA); Idaho: St. Maries; Maine: Auburn, Bethel, Poland (GS), West Paris; Montana: Alder, Helena (S); New

Hampshire: Grafton (I); New Mexico: Dixon; North Carolina (*): Almond, Boone (SA), Cherokee, Chimney Rock (SA), Franklin (5), Hiddenite, Highlands, Little Switzerland (2), Marshall, Spruce Pine (3) (FT); Nevada: Ely; Virginia: Virginia City; Washington: Ravensdale (GS)

**Almandine garnets**  Maine: Poland (GS); Nevada: Ely

**Pyrope garnets**  North Carolina: Franklin

**Rhodolite garnets**  North Carolina: Franklin (5)

**Sagittarius (November 22–December 21) Emerald**  Georgia: Cleveland, Dahlonega (SA); North Carolina (*): Cherokee, Franklin, Hiddenite, Little Switzerland (2), Marion, Spruce Pine (2)

**Crabtree emerald**  North Carolina: Spruce Pine

**Capricorn (December 22–January 21) Chalcedony**  Arizona: Safford; New Mexico: Deming

**Blue chalcedony**  Nevada: Sun Valley (GS)

# Some Publications on Gems and Minerals

## Lapidary Journal

Main Office
300 Chesterfield Parkway, Suite 100
Malvern, PA 19355
Phone: (610) 232-5770
Subscriptions: (800) 676-4336
www.lapidaryjournal.com

## Rocks & Minerals

Heldref Publications
1319 18th Street, NW
Washington, DC 20036-1802
Subscriptions: (800) 365-9753

## Rock & Gem

c/o Miller Magazines, Inc.
Maple Court, Suite 232
Ventura, CA 93003-3517
www.rockngem.com

## Gold Prospector

Gold Prospectors Association of America, Inc.
P.O. Box 891509
Temecula, CA 92589
Phone: (951) 699-4749
www.goldprospectors.org

Other sources of information are local and regional rock, gem, and mineral clubs and federations, and rock, gem, and mineral shows. Many times clubs offer field trips and some shows have collecting trips associated with their annual event.

# Send Us Your Feedback

## Disclaimer

The authors have made every reasonable effort to obtain accurate information for this guide. However, much of the information in the book is based on material provided by the sites and has not been verified independently. The information given here does not represent recommendations, but merely a listing of information. The authors and publisher accept no liability for any accident or loss incurred when readers are patronizing the establishments listed herein. The authors and publisher accept no liability for errors or omissions. Since sites may shut down or change their hours of operations or fees without advance notice, please call the site before your visit for confirmation before planning your trip.

The authors would appreciate being informed of changes, additions, or deletions that should be made to this guide. To that end, a form is attached, which can be filled out and mailed to the authors for use in future editions of the guide.

## Have We Missed Your Mine or Museum?

This is a project with a national scope, based on extensive literature search, phone and mail inquiry, and personal investigation. However, we are dealing with a business in which many owners are retiring or closing and selling their sites. In addition, many of the mines, guide services, and smaller museums have limited publicity, known more by word of mouth than by publication. Thus, it is possible that your operation or one you have visited was not included in this guide. Please let us know if you own or operate a mine, guide service, or museum, or have visited a mine, guide service, or museum that is not in the guide. It will be considered for inclusion in the next edition of the guide. Send updates to:

Treasure Hunter's Guides
GemStone Press
Route 4, Sunset Farm Offices
P.O. Box 237
Woodstock, VT 05091

## Do You Have a Rockhounding Story to Share?

If you have a special story about a favorite dig site, send it in for consideration for use in the next edition of the guide.

## A Request to Mines and Museums:

For sites already included in this guide, we request that you put us on your annual mailing list so that we may have an updated copy of your information.

## Notes on Museums

In this guide we have included listings of museums with noteworthy gem, mineral, or rock collections. We particularly tried to find local museums displaying gems or minerals native to the area where they are located. This list is by no means complete, and if you feel we missed an important listing, let us know by completing the following form. Since these guides focus specifically on gems and minerals, only those exhibits have been recognized in the museum listings, and we do not mention any collection or exhibits of fossils.

## READER'S CONTRIBUTION

I would like to supply the following information for possible inclusion in the next edition of *The Treasure Hunter's Guide*:

**Type of entry:**  ☐ fee dig  ☐ guide service  ☐ museum  ☐ mine tour
☐ annual event

**This is a:**  ☐ new entry  ☐ entry currently in the guide

**Nature of info:**  ☐ addition  ☐ change  ☐ deletion

*Please describe (brochure and additional info may be attached):*

_____

_____

_____

_____

Please supply the following in case we need to contact you regarding your information:

Name: _____

Address: _____

_____

_____

Phone: ( ) _____

E-mail: _____

Date: _____

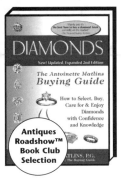

## DIAMONDS, 2ND EDITION:
## THE ANTOINETTE MATLINS BUYING GUIDE
*How to Select, Buy, Care for & Enjoy Diamonds with Confidence and Knowledge*
*by* Antoinette Matlins, P.G.

Practical, comprehensive, and easy to understand, this book includes price guides for old and new cuts and for fancy-color, treated, and synthetic diamonds. **Explains in detail** how to read diamond grading reports and offers important advice for after buying a diamond. **The "unofficial bible" for all diamond buyers who want to get the most for their money.**

6" x 9", 220 pp., 12 full-color pages & many b/w illustrations and photos; index
Quality Paperback Original, ISBN 0-943763-46-0 **$18.99**

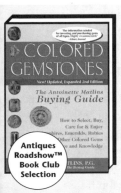

## COLORED GEMSTONES, 2ND EDITION:
## THE ANTOINETTE MATLINS BUYING GUIDE
*How to Select, Buy, Care for & Enjoy Sapphires, Emeralds, Rubies and Other Colored Gems with Confidence and Knowledge*
*by* Antoinette Matlins, P.G.

This practical, comprehensive, easy-to-understand guide **provides in depth** all the information you need to buy colored gems with confidence. Includes price guides for popular gems, opals, and synthetic stones. Provides examples of gemstone grading reports and offers important advice for after buying a gemstone. **Shows anyone shopping for colored gemstones how to get the most for their money.**

6" x 9", 224 pp., 24 full-color pages & many b/w illustrations and photos; index
Quality Paperback Original, ISBN 0-943763-45-2 **$18.99**

## THE PEARL BOOK, 3RD EDITION:
## THE DEFINITIVE BUYING GUIDE
*How to Select, Buy, Care for & Enjoy Pearls*
*by* Antoinette Matlins, P.G.

**COMPREHENSIVE • EASY TO READ • PRACTICAL**

This comprehensive, authoritative guide tells readers everything they need to know about pearls to fully understand and appreciate them, and avoid any unexpected—and costly—disappointments, now and in future generations.

- A journey into the rich history and romance surrounding pearls.
- The five factors that determine pearl value & judging pearl quality.
- What to look for, what to look out for: How to spot fakes. Treatments.
- Differences between natural, cultured and imitation pearls, and ways to separate them.
- Comparisons of all types of pearls, in every size and color, from every pearl-producing country.

6" x 9", 232 pp., 16 full-color pages & over 250 color and b/w illustrations and photos; index
Quality Paperback, ISBN 0-943763-35-5 **$19.99**

**FOR CREDIT CARD ORDERS CALL 800-962-4544** (8:30AM–5:30PM ET Monday–Friday)
*Available from your bookstore or directly from the publisher.* **TRY YOUR BOOKSTORE FIRST.**

# The "Unofficial Bible" for the Gem & Jewelry Buyer

## JEWELRY & GEMS:
### THE BUYING GUIDE, 6TH EDITION

**NEW CHAPTER ON
Antique and Period
Jewelry**

*How to Buy Diamonds, Pearls, Colored Gemstones,
Gold & Jewelry with Confidence and Knowledge*
by Antoinette Matlins, P.G., *and* A. C. Bonanno, F.G.A., P.G., A.S.A.
*—over 400,000 copies in print—*

**Learn the tricks of the trade from** *insiders:* How to buy diamonds,
pearls, precious and other popular colored gems with confidence
and knowledge. More than just a buying guide . . . discover what's
available and what choices you have, what determines quality as
well as cost, what questions to ask before you buy and what to get
in writing. Easy to read and understand. Excellent for staff training.

6" x 9",  336 pp., 16 full-color pages & over 200 color and b/w illustrations and photos; index
Quality Paperback, ISBN 0-943763-44-4  **$19.99;** Hardcover, ISBN 0-943763-47-9  **$24.99**

## • COMPREHENSIVE • EASY TO READ • PRACTICAL •
### ENGAGEMENT & WEDDING RINGS, 3RD EDITION

by Antoinette Matlins, P.G., *and* A. C. Bonanno, F.G.A., A.S.A., M.G.A.

Tells **everything you need to know to design, select, buy and
enjoy that "perfect" ring** and to truly experience the wonder and
excitement that should be part of it.

Updated, expanded, filled with valuable information.

*Engagement & Wedding Rings,* 3rd Ed., will help you make the *right*
choice. You will discover romantic traditions behind engagement
and wedding rings, how to select the right style and design for *you*, tricks to get
what you want on a budget, ways to add new life to an "heirloom," what to do to protect
yourself against fraud, and much more.

Dazzling 16-page color section of rings showing antique to contemporary designs.
Over 400 illustrations and photographs. Index.
6" x 9", 320 pp., Quality Paperback, ISBN 0-943763-41-X  **$18.95**

## JEWELRY & GEMS AT AUCTION

*The Definitive Guide to Buying & Selling
at the Auction House & on Internet Auction Sites*
by Antoinette Matlins, P.G.
*with contributions by* Jill Newman

As buying and selling at auctions—both traditional auction houses
and "virtual" Internet auctions—moves into the mainstream,
**consumers need to know how to "play the game."** There are
treasures to be had and money to be saved and made, but buying
and selling at auction offers unique risks as well as unique
opportunities. This book makes available—for the first time—detailed information on
how to buy and sell jewelry and gems at auction without making costly mistakes.

6" x 9", 352 pp., fully illustrated
Quality Paperback Original, ISBN 0-943763-29-0  **$19.95**

# Now You Can Have the "Professional's Advantage"!
## With Your OWN Jeweler's Loupe—
# The Essential "TOOL OF THE TRADE"!

Personally selected by the authors, this valuable jeweler's aid is *now available to the consumer* from GemStone Press. And GemStone Press includes, FREE, a copy of "The Professional's Advantage: How to Use the Loupe and What to Look For," a $5.00 value, written with the jewelry buyer in mind. You can now *have more fun while shopping and make your choice with greater confidence*. This is not just a magnifying glass. It is specially made to be used to examine jewelry. It will help you to—

- *Enjoy* the inner beauty of the gem as well as the outer beauty.
- *Protect yourself*—see scratches, chips, or cracks that reduce the value of a stone or make it vulnerable to greater damage.
- *Prevent loss*—spot weak prongs that may break and cause the stone to fall from the setting.
- *Avoid bad cutting*, poor proportioning and poor symmetry.
- *Identify the telltale signs* of glass or imitation.
- . . . *And much more, as revealed in "The Professional's Advantage"!*

You'll love it. You'll enjoy looking at gems and jewelry up close—it makes this special experience even more exciting. And sometimes, as one of our readers recently wrote:

*"Just having the loupe and looking like I knew how to use it changed the way I was treated."*

## CALL NOW AND WE'LL RUSH THE LOUPE TO YOU.
### FOR TOLL-FREE CREDIT CARD ORDERS:
# 800-962-4544

| Item | Quantity | Price Each | TOTAL |
|---|---|---|---|
| Standard 10X Triplet Loupe | _____ | $29.00 | = $_____ |
| Bausch & Lomb 10X Triplet Loupe | _____ | $44.00 | = $_____ |
| "The Professional's Advantage" Booklet | 1 per Loupe | $ 5.00 | = Free |
| Insurance/Packing/Shipping in the U.S.* | 1st Loupe | $ 7.95 | = $ 7.95 |
| *Outside U.S.: Specify shipping method (insured) and provide a credit card number for payment. | Each add'l | $ 3.00 | = $_____ |
| | | TOTAL: | $_____ |

Check enclosed for $_____ (Payable to: GEMSTONE PRESS)
Charge my credit card: ❑ Visa ❑ MasterCard
Name on Card _____
Cardholder Address: Street _____
City/State/Zip _____ E-mail _____
Credit Card # _____ Exp. Date _____
Signature _____ Phone (____)_____
*Please send to:* ❑ Same as Above ❑ Address Below
Name _____
Street _____
City/State/Zip _____ Phone (____)_____

**TOTAL SATISFACTION GUARANTEE**

If for any reason you're not completely delighted with your purchase, return it in resellable condition within 30 days for a full refund.

*Phone, mail, fax, or e-mail orders to:*
GEMSTONE PRESS, Sunset Farm Offices, Rte. 4, P.O. Box 237, Woodstock, VT 05091
*Tel:* (802) 457-4000 • *Fax:* (802) 457-4004 • *Credit Card Orders:* (800) 962-4544
sales@gemstonepress.com • www.gemstonepress.com
Generous Discounts on Quantity Orders

Prices subject to change

ASK ABOUT OTHER GEM ID INSTRUMENTS — REFRACTOMETERS • DICHROSCOPES • MICROSCOPES • AND MORE
**FOR CREDIT CARD ORDERS CALL 800-962-4544** (8:30AM–5:30PM ET Monday–Friday)

# Do You Really Know What You're Buying? Is It Fake or Is It Real?

*The companion book to*
**Jewelry & Gems: The Buying Guide**

If You Aren't Sure, Order Now—

## NEW, REVISED, EXPANDED EDITION
## THE ONLY BOOK OF ITS KIND
# GEM IDENTIFICATION MADE EASY, 3RD EDITION

*A Hands-On Guide to More Confident Buying & Selling*
by Antoinette Matlins, P.G., *and* A. C. Bonanno, F.G.A., A.S.A., M.G.A.

**Antiques Roadshow™ Book Club Selection**

The only book that explains in non-technical terms how to use pocket, portable and laboratory instruments to identify diamonds and colored gems and to separate them from imitations and "look-alikes."

The book's approach is direct and practical, and its style is **easy to understand.** In fact, with this easy-to-use guide, *anyone* can begin to master gem identification.

Using a simple, step-by-step system, the authors explain the proper use of essential but uncomplicated instruments that will do the identification tasks, what to look for gemstone-by-gemstone, and how to set up a basic lab at modest cost. **Three of the instruments are inexpensive, portable, pocket instruments that, when used together, can identify almost 85% of all precious and popular stones.**

*Including Complete and Easy Instructions:*

**NEW Gems**
**NEW Treatments**
**NEW Synthetics**
**NEW Instruments**

◆ Setting Up a Basic Lab
◆ Description of Each Instrument — What It Will Show & How to Use It
**NEW!** SSEF Diamond-Type Spotter • Electronic Diamond Dual Tester • Darkfield Loupe • Synthetic Emerald Filters • Immersion Cell • Synthetic Diamond Detector Loupe • Chelsea Filter • Refractometer • Ultraviolet Lamp • Microscope • Spectroscope • Polariscope • Dichroscope
◆ **Antique and Estate Jewelry** — *The True Test for the Gem Detective* Dyeing • Composite Stones • Foil Backing • Substitutions
◆ **Appendices:** Charts and Tables of Gemstone Properties, Schools, Laboratories, Associations, Publications and Recommended Reading

As entertaining as it is informative. Essential for gem lovers, jewelers, antique dealers, collectors, investors and hobbyists. **"THE BOOK YOU CAN'T DO WITHOUT."** —*Rapaport Diamond Report*

6" x 9", 372 pp., with more than 150 photographs and illustrations, 75 in full color; index
Hardcover, ISBN 0-943763-34-7 **$36.95**

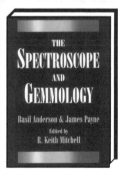

# THE SPECTROSCOPE AND GEMMOLOGY
*Ed. by* R. Keith Mitchell, F.G.A.

**"Well written and illustrated. An invaluable work for anyone involved in gemstone identification."**
—*Choice, Science & Technology*

The first book devoted exclusively to the spectroscope and its use in gemstone identification, this comprehensive reference includes the history and development of spectroscopy; discussion of the nature of absorption·spectra and the absorption spectra of solids and gem minerals; the many uses of the spectroscope and the spectrophotometer; light sources and the causes of color; absorption in synthetic gemstones; and more. Indispensable for professional and amateur gemologists and students of gemology.

6" x 9", 288 pp., over 75 b/w illustrations; index
Hardcover, ISBN 0-943763-18-5 **$69.95**

**FOR CREDIT CARD ORDERS CALL 800-962-4544** (8:30AM–5:30PM ET Monday–Friday)
*Available from your bookstore or directly from the publisher.* **TRY YOUR BOOKSTORE FIRST.**

# Buy Your "Tools of the Trade"...

## Gem Identification Instruments directly from *GemStone Press*

Whatever instrument you need, GemStone Press can help.
Use our convenient order form, or contact us directly for assistance.

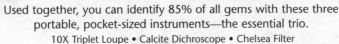

### Complete Pocket Instrument Set
# SPECIAL SAVINGS!
### BUY THIS ESSENTIAL TRIO AND SAVE 12%

Used together, you can identify 85% of all gems with these three
portable, pocket-sized instruments—the essential trio.

10X Triplet Loupe • Calcite Dichroscope • Chelsea Filter

**Pocket Instrument Set:**

**Premium:** With Bausch & Lomb 10X Loupe • RosGem Dichroscope • Chelsea Filter    **only $197.95**

**Deluxe:** With Bausch & Lomb 10X Loupe • EZview Dichroscope • Chelsea Filter    **only $179.95**

| ITEM / QUANTITY | PRICE EA.* | TOTAL $ |
|---|---|---|
| **Pocket Instrument Sets** | | |
| _____ **Premium:** With Bausch & Lomb 10X Loupe • RosGem Dichroscope • Chelsea Filter | $197.95 | $ _____ |
| _____ **Deluxe:** With Bausch & Lomb 10X Loupe • EZview Dichroscope • Chelsea Filter | $179.95 | _____ |
| **Loupes—Professional Jeweler's 10X Triplet Loupes** | | |
| _____ Bausch & Lomb 10X Triplet Loupe | $44.00 | _____ |
| _____ Standard 10X Triplet Loupe | $29.00 | _____ |
| _____ Darkfield Loupe | $58.95 | _____ |
| • Spot filled diamonds, identify inclusions in colored gemstones. Operates with mini maglite (optional). | | |
| **Analyzer** | | |
| _____ Gem Analyzer (RosGem) | $299.00 | _____ |
| • Combines Darkfield Loupe, Polariscope, and Immersion Cell. Operates with mini maglite (optional). | | |
| **Calcite Dichroscopes** | | |
| _____ Dichroscope (RosGem) | $135.00 | _____ |
| _____ Dichroscope (EZview) | $115.00 | _____ |
| **Color Filters** | | |
| _____ Chelsea Filter | $44.95 | _____ |
| _____ Synthetic Emerald Filter Set (Hanneman) | $32.00 | _____ |
| _____ Tanzanite Filter (Hanneman) | $28.00 | _____ |
| _____ Bead Buyer's & Parcel Picker's Filter Set (Hanneman) | $24.00 | _____ |
| **Diamond Testers and Tweezers** | | |
| _____ SSEF Diamond-Type Spotter | $150.00 | _____ |
| _____ Diamondnite Dual Tester | $269.00 | _____ |
| _____ Diamond Tweezers/Locking | $10.65 | _____ |
| _____ Diamond Tweezers/Non-Locking | $7.80 | _____ |
| **Jewelry Cleaners** | | |
| _____ Ionic Cleaner—Home size model | $69.95 | _____ |
| _____ Ionic Solution—16 oz. bottle | $20.00 | _____ |

# Buy Your *"Tools of the Trade..."*

## Gem Identification Instruments directly from *GemStone Press*

Whatever instrument you need, GemStone Press can help.
Use our convenient order form, or contact us directly for assistance.

| ITEM / QUANTITY | PRICE EA.* | TOTAL $ |
|---|---|---|
| **Lamps—Ultraviolet & High Intensity** | | |
| _____ Small Longwave/Shortwave (UVP) | $72.00 | _____ |
| _____ Large Longwave/Shortwave (UVP) | $199.95 | _____ |
| _____ Viewing Cabinet for Large Lamp (UVP) | $175.00 | _____ |
| _____ **Purchase Large Lamp & Cabinet together and save $35.00** | $339.95 | _____ |
| _____ SSEF High-Intensity Shortwave Illuminator | $499.00 | _____ |
| • For Use with the SSEF Diamond-Type Spotter | | |
| **Other Light Sources** | | |
| _____ Solitaire Maglite | $11.00 | _____ |
| _____ Mini Maglite | $15.00 | _____ |
| _____ Flex Light | $29.95 | _____ |
| **Refractometers** | | |
| _____ Precision Pocket Refractometer (RosGem RFA 322) | $625.00 | |
| • operates with solitaire maglite (additional—see above) | | |
| _____ Refractive Index Liquid 1.81—10 gram | $59.95 | _____ |
| **Spectroscopes** | | |
| _____ Spectroscope—Pocket-sized model (OPL) | $98.00 | _____ |
| _____ Spectroscope—Desk model w/stand (OPL) | $235.00 | _____ |
| **Scale** | | |
| _____ GemPro50 Carat Scale | $174.95 | _____ |

**Shipping/Insurance per order in the U.S.: $7.95 first item,** SHIPPING/INS. $_____
**$3.00 each add'l item; $10.95 total for pocket instrument set.**

Outside the U.S.: Please specify *insured* shipping method you prefer
and provide a credit card number for payment. **TOTAL $** _____ **

Check enclosed for $ _____ (Payable to: GEMSTONE PRESS)
Charge my credit card: ❑ Visa ❑ MasterCard
Name on Card _____ Phone (_____)_____
Cardholder Address: Street _____
City/State/Zip _____ E-mail _____
Credit Card #_____ Exp. Date _____
Signature _____ CID # _____
*Please send to:* ❑ Same as Above ❑ Address Below
Name _____
Street _____
City/State/Zip _____ Phone (_____)_____

*Phone, mail, fax, or e-mail orders to:*

**GEMSTONE PRESS, P.O. Box 237, Woodstock, VT 05091**
*Tel:* (802) 457-4000 • *Fax:* (802) 457-4004
*Credit Card Orders:* (800) 962-4544 (8:30AM–5:30PM ET Monday–Friday)
**sales@gemstonepress.com • www.gemstonepress.com**
**Generous Discounts on Quantity Orders**

**TOTAL SATISFACTION GUARANTEE**
If for any reason you're not completely delighted
with your purchase, return it in resellable condition
within 30 days for a full refund.

*Prices, manufacturing specifications, and terms subject to change
without notice. Orders accepted subject to availability.
**All orders must be prepaid by credit card, money order or check
in U.S. funds drawn on a U.S. bank.

# CAMEOS OLD & NEW, 3RD EDITION
*by* Anna M. Miller, G.G.

Newly updated and expanded, *Cameos Old & New,* 3rd Ed., is a **concise, easy-to-understand guide** enabling anyone—from beginner to antique dealer—to recognize and evaluate quality and value in cameos, and avoid the pitfalls of purchasing mediocre pieces, fakes and forgeries.

6" x 9", 312 pp., over 300 photographs and illustrations, 130 in full color; index
Quality Paperback, ISBN 0-943763-36-3 **$19.95**

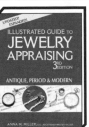

# ILLUSTRATED GUIDE TO JEWELRY APPRAISING,
**3RD EDITION** • *Antique, Period, Modern*
*by* Anna M. Miller, G.G., Registered Master Valuer

This beautifully illustrated guide **provides step-by-step instruction** in jewelry identification and dating, reviews the responsibilities of the appraiser, and describes in detail virtually every style of antique and period jewelry for the hobbyist and serious collector alike.

8½" x 11", 224 pp., over 150 photographs and illustrations; index
Hardcover, ISBN 0-943763-42-8 **$39.99**

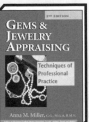

# GEMS & JEWELRY APPRAISING, 2ND EDITION
*Techniques of Professional Practice*
*by* Anna M. Miller, G.G., Registered Master Valuer

The **premier guide to the standards, procedures and ethics of appraising gems, jewelry and other valuables.** *Gems & Jewelry Appraising* offers all the information that jewelers, gemologists and students will need to establish an appraisal business, handle various kinds of appraisals and provide an accurate, verifiable estimate of value.

8½" x 11", 256 pp., over 130 photographs and illustrations; index
Hardcover, ISBN 0-943763-10-X **$39.95**

# TREASURE HUNTER'S GEM & MINERAL GUIDES TO THE U.S.A.
## 3RD EDITIONS
*Where & How to Dig, Pan and Mine Your Own Gems & Minerals*
**—IN 4 REGIONAL VOLUMES—**
*by* Kathy J. Rygle *and* Stephen F. Pedersen • *Preface by* Antoinette Matlins, P.G., *author of* Gem Identification Made Easy

From rubies, opals and gold, to emeralds, aquamarine and diamonds, each guide offers **state-by-state details on more than 250 gems and minerals** and the affordable "fee dig" sites where they can be found. Each guide covers:

- **Equipment & Clothing:** What you need and where to find it.
- **Mining Techniques:** Step-by-step instructions.
- **Gem and Mineral Sites:** Directions & maps, hours, fees, and more.
- **Museums and Mine Tours**

All guides: 6" x 9", Quality Paperback Original, Illustrations, maps & photos, indexes. **$14.99 each**

**Northeast** (CT, DC, DE, IL, IN, MA, MD, ME, MI, NH, NJ, NY, OH, PA, RI, VT, WI)
208 pp., ISBN 0-943763-49-5
**Northwest** (AK, IA, ID, MN, MT, ND, NE, OR, SD, WA, WY)
176 pp., ISBN 0-943763-48-7
**Southeast** (AL, AR, FL, GA, KY, LA, MO, MS, NC, SC, TN, VA, WV)
192 pp., ISBN 0-943763-51-7
**Southwest** (AZ, CA, CO, HI, KS, NM, NV, OK, TX, UT)
208 pp., ISBN 0-943763-50-9

*Please send me:*

**CAMEOS OLD & NEW, 3RD EDITION**
_____ copies at $19.95 (Quality Paperback) *plus s/h\**

**COLORED GEMSTONES, 2ND EDITION: THE ANTOINETTE MATLINS BUYING GUIDE**
_____ copies at $18.99 (Quality Paperback) *plus s/h\**

**DIAMONDS, 2ND EDITION: THE ANTOINETTE MATLINS BUYING GUIDE**
_____ copies at $18.99 (Quality Paperback) *plus s/h\**

**ENGAGEMENT & WEDDING RINGS, 3RD EDITION: THE DEFINITIVE BUYING GUIDE**
_____ copies at $18.95 (Quality Paperback) *plus s/h\**

**GEM IDENTIFICATION MADE EASY, 3RD EDITION:**
**A HANDS-ON GUIDE TO MORE CONFIDENT BUYING & SELLING**
_____ copies at $36.95 (Hardcover) *plus s/h\**

**GEMS & JEWELRY APPRAISING, 2ND EDITION**
_____ copies at $39.95 (Hardcover) *plus s/h\**

**ILLUSTRATED GUIDE TO JEWELRY APPRAISING, 3RD EDITION**
_____ copies at $39.99 (Hardcover) *plus s/h\**

**JEWELRY & GEMS AT AUCTION: THE DEFINITIVE GUIDE TO BUYING & SELLING**
**AT THE AUCTION HOUSE & ON INTERNET AUCTION SITES**
_____ copies at $19.95 (Quality Paperback) *plus s/h\**

**JEWELRY & GEMS, 6TH EDITION: THE BUYING GUIDE**
_____ copies at $19.99 (Quality Paperback) *plus s/h\**
_____ copies at $24.99 (Hardcover) *plus s/h\**

**THE PEARL BOOK, 3RD EDITION: THE DEFINITIVE BUYING GUIDE**
_____ copies at $19.99 (Quality Paperback) *plus s/h\**

**THE SPECTROSCOPE AND GEMMOLOGY**
_____ copies at $69.95 (Hardcover) *plus s/h\**

**TREASURE HUNTER'S GEM & MINERAL GUIDES TO THE U.S.A., 3RD EDITIONS:**
**WHERE & HOW TO DIG, PAN AND MINE YOUR OWN GEMS & MINERALS—**
**IN 4 REGIONAL VOLUMES** $14.99 per copy (Quality Paperback) *plus s/h\**
\_\_\_\_\_ copies of NE States \_\_\_\_\_ copies of SE States \_\_\_\_\_ copies of NW States \_\_\_\_\_ copies of SW States

\* In U.S.: Shipping/Handling: $3.95 for 1st book, $2.00 each additional book.
Outside U.S.: Specify shipping method (insured) and provide a credit card number for payment.

---

Check enclosed for $_____ (Payable to: GEMSTONE Press)
Charge my credit card: ❑ Visa ❑ MasterCard
Name on Card (PRINT) _____ Phone (\_\_\_\_)_____
Cardholder Address: Street _____
City/State/Zip _____ E-mail _____
Credit Card # _____ Exp. Date _____
Signature _____ CID # _____
*Please send to:* ❑ Same as Above ❑ Address Below
Name (PRINT) _____
Street _____
City/State/Zip _____ Phone (\_\_\_\_)_____

---

**TOTAL SATISFACTION GUARANTEE**
If for any reason you're not completely delighted with your purchase, return it in resellable condition within 30 days for a full refund.

*Phone, mail, fax, or e-mail orders to:*
**GEMSTONE PRESS,** Sunset Farm Offices,
Rte. 4, P.O. Box 237, Woodstock, VT 05091
*Tel:* (802) 457-4000 • *Fax:* (802) 457-4004
*Credit Card Orders:* (800) 962-4544
(8:30AM–5:30PM ET Monday–Friday)
sales@gemstonepress.com • www.gemstonepress.com
**Generous Discounts on Quantity Orders**

Prices subject to change

## Try Your Bookstore First